EMOTIONAL INTELLIGENCE II

People Smart Role Models

Emerson Klees

Cameo Press

Rochester, New York

For information, write:

Cameo Press
P. O. Box 18131
Rochester, New York 14618

Library of Congress Control Number 2012947505

ISBN 978-1-891046-15-5

Printed in the United States of America
9 8 7 6 5 4 3 2 1

TABLE OF CONTENTS

PREFACE

The purpose of this book is to use role models from history to illustrate the importance of people skills in achieving success. Being smart, if defined as having a high Intelligence Quotient (IQ), certainly contributes to achievement, but the Emotional Quotient (EQ), the measure of Emotional Intelligence, is a more important factor in being successful.

It has been determined that IQ contributes approximately 20% to success, leaving approximately 80% to other factors, such as EQ. Furthermore, the traits that make up Emotional Intelligence, including emotional control, empathy, and perseverance, are factors that can be improved, unlike IQ, which remains relatively fixed from young adulthood.

We all have acquaintances and friends who may not be the brightest or the most highly educated people that we know, but who have achieved success in life, perhaps notable success. They are probably doing what they want to be doing for a career and what they are good at doing. They may have accomplished their goals by recognizing their weaknesses and strengths and by working hard. It is likely that they have addressed their weaknesses by teaming up with a person or persons with complementary strengths.

The principal goal of this book is to aid the reader in understanding the elements of Emotional Intelligence, potentially allowing him or her to become more of a "people person." If we can identify our shortcomings, whether they are insufficient optimism, lack of assertiveness, poor motivation, or other factors, then we can strive to improve our EQ.

A debt is acknowledged to other authors for their work on the subject of Emotional Intelligence, particularly Daniel Goleman, Harvey Deutschendorf, and Mel Silberman.

PROLOGUE

"Emotional Intelligence refers to an array of attributes and tools that enables us to deal with the pressures and demands of our environment. Emotional Intelligence has been referred to as common sense or advanced common sense. Street smarts is another term that has been used in connection with Emotional Intelligence."

Harvey Deutschendorf, *The Other Kind of Smart*

A principal goal in life is to be happy. We may have wealth and many possessions, but if we aren't happy, what is it all worth? One of the key factors of happiness is success. If we are successful, we have a better chance of being happy. Nevertheless, being successful is not a guarantee of happiness.

We would like to know how to be successful at work and in our family relationships in order to have more satisfying and fulfilling lives. In addition to success with a career and at home, higher-level purposes exist: helping others and making the world a better place in which to live. Helping others contributes to our own happiness. Emotional Intelligence is a heavy contributor to our attainment of success and happiness.

According to Daniel Goleman in *Emotional Intelligence,* "[Some] subscribe to a narrow view of intelligence, arguing that IQ is a genetic given that cannot be changed by life experience, that our destiny is largely fixed by these aptitudes. That argument ignores the more challenging question: What can change that will help [us] fare better in life? What factors are at play, for example, when people of high IQ flounder and those of modest IQ do surprisingly well?

"The difference quite often lies in the abilities called Emotional Intelligence, which includes self-control, zeal, and persistence, and the ability to motivate oneself. And these skills . . . can be taught, giving [us] a better chance to use whatever intellectual potential the genetic lottery has given [us]."

Also, according to Goleman, "Academic intelligence has little to do with emotional life. The brightest among us can flounder on the shoals of unbridled passions and unruly impulse; people with high IQs can be stunningly poor pilots of their private lives. One of psychology's open secrets is the relatively inability of grades, IQ, or SAT scores, despite their popular mystique, to predict unerringly who will succeed in life.

"To be sure, there is a relationship between IQ and life circumstances for large groups as a whole; many people with low IQs end up in menial jobs and those with high IQs tend to become well-paid—but by no means always. There are widespread exceptions to the rule that IQ predicts success—many (or more) exceptions than cases that fit the rule."

All of us know of people who dropped out of high school or who decided not to go to college who became very successful in life, perhaps as contractors or entrepreneurs. We probably also know individuals who were at the top of their class academically but who never really found their way in life.

The attributes of Emotional Intelligence, including motivation, leadership, negotiation / persuasion, and conflict resolution, are important in the workplace in many ways. Emotional Intelligence and productivity are directly related. Studies conducted in the workplace have indicated that from 27 to 45 percent of success on the job is determined by our Emotional Intelligence. In an organization, ability to work with others is of the utmost importance. People skills contribute heavily to working well with others. Being a "people person" is as important in the workplace as it is in life itself.

Some of the biographical sketches in this book are based on profiles in earlier Human Values Series books:

The Drive to Succeed: Role Models of Motivation
Entrepreneurs in History—Success vs. Failure:
    Entrepreneurial Role Models
One Plus One Equals Three— Pairing Man / Woman Strengths:
    Role Models of Teamwork
Staying With It: Role Models of Perseverance
The Will to Stay With It: Role Models of Determination

These books have end notes and comprehensive bibliographies for further reading.

INTRODUCTION

"Emotional Intelligence refers to the capacity for recognizing our own feelings and those of others, for motivating ourselves, and for managing emotions well in ourselves and in our relationships. It describes abilities distinct from, but complementary to, academic intelligence, the purely cognitive capacities measured by IQ. Many people who are book smart but lack emotional intelligence end up working for people who have lower IQs than they but who excel in Emotional Intelligence skills."

Daniel Goleman, *Working with Emotional Intelligence*

Emotional Intelligence has been widely written about, with some variations in the attributes that make up EQ. In *Working with Emotional Intelligence,* author Daniel Goleman identified five basic emotional and social competencies:

- Self-awareness: Having a realistic assessment of our own abilities and a well-grounded sense of self-confidence
- Self-regulation: Handling our emotions so that they facilitate rather than interfere with the task at hand
- Motivation: Using our deepest preferences to move and guide us toward our goals
- Empathy: Sensing what people are feeling, being able to take their perspective
- Social skills: Handling emotions in relationships well and accurately reading social situations and networks; using these skills to persuade and lead, negotiate and settle disputes, for cooperation and teamwork

In *People Smart,* Mel Silberman identifies the skills involved in being people smart:

- Understanding people
- Expressing yourself clearly
- Asserting your needs
- Exchanging feedback
- Influencing others
- Resolving conflict
- Being a team player
- Shifting gears / flexibility

PART I

Role models in Part I of this book illustrate the following traits of Emotional Intelligence:

Perseverance	Social Responsibility
Empathy	Motivation
Optimism	Assertiveness
Persuasion / Negotiation	Relationships
Leadership	Teamwork
Emotional Control	

Perseverance

Perseverance is a critical factor in accomplishment and success. Intelligence alone doesn't guarantee success. Many brilliant men and women in history didn't gain the same distinction as their peers with less intelligence who worked hard and persevered. Frequently, an individual with superior perseverance and average intelligence out-performs one with superior intelligence and average or below average perseverance. As David G. Ryans observes in "The Meaning of Persistence" in the *Journal of General Psychology*: "Persistence and success are inseparably bound together in the popular mind, and rightly so. For achievement through aptitude or ability alone is undoubtedly the exception rather than the rule. Most tasks demand more than brilliance."

Empathy

In *The Other Kind of Smart,* Harvey Deutschendorf observes: "Empathy means being able to accurately read where other people are at emotionally. It means being able to get below the words others are saying to sense the underlying feelings. To do that, we must be able to pick up not only the words but also the force and tone with which they are said. Along with this, we need to take into account facial expression, posture, and other indicators that will give us valuable clues into the person's emotional state." Empathy should not be confused with sympathy, which brings out our own feelings as opposed to reading the feelings of others.

Optimism

Daniel Goleman in *Emotional Intelligence* notes: "Optimism, like hope, means having a strong expectation that, in general, things will turn out all right, despite setbacks and frustrations. From the standpoint of Emotional Intelligence, optimism is an attitude that buffers people against falling into apathy, hopelessness, or depression in the face of tough going. And, as with hope, its near cousin, optimism pays dividends in life (providing of course it is realistic optimism)."

Persuasion / Negotiation

In *People Smart,* Mel Silberman observes: "Influencing others has to do with getting them to be receptive to your views, advice and recommendations. It is not about your getting them to admit that you are right or forcing them to do as you wish. You can't make someone see the world as you see it, but you can sometimes open their mind to new attitudes and effective courses of action. Unfortunately, many people are intent on making people over in their own image."

Leadership

Leadership is not the art of dominating people but that of persuading them to work toward common goals. In *The Other Kind of Smart,* Harvey Deutschendorf notes: "When employee satisfaction levels within organizations have been studied, dissatisfaction with leadership has come out as the most common reason for leaving the workplace. Leaders have a tremendous ability to influence the staff under them in both positive and negative ways. Effective leaders are able to use their people skills to encourage, motivate, and get the most from their employees, while ineffective ones can cause morale and productivity to plummet."

Emotional Control

According to Daniel Goleman in *Emotional Intelligence,* "Handling feelings so they are appropriate is an ability that builds on self-awareness . . . recognizing a feeling as it happens—the keystone of emotional intelligence—the ability to monitor feelings from moment to moment is crucial to psychological insight and and self-understanding. . . . [Managing emotions involves] the capacity to soothe oneself, to shake off rampant anxiety, gloom, or irritability. . . . People who are poor in this ability are constantly battling feelings of distress, while those who excel in it can bounce back far more quickly from life's setbacks and upsets."

Social Responsibility

In *The Other Kind of Smart,* Harvey Deutschendorf notes: "We are all socially responsible to the degree that we see ourselves as being part of something larger than ourselves. Socially responsible people have a sense of duty to make the world a better place in which to live . . . work that helps others brings us satisfaction and happiness. [A national opinion survey] has found that the people who reported the highest level of happiness and satisfaction were those that had jobs serving other people. The benefits of helping others are enormous."

Motivation

Abraham Maslow, who describes his theory of motivation in *Motivation and Personality,* outlines a hierarchy of needs in which people are concerned with needs at a higher level only when those at a lower level have been satisfied. The lowest level is the fulfillment of physiological needs, such as those for physical survival—food, drink, and shelter. The second level comprises safety needs, such as security, stability, protection, and freedom from anxiety and fear. Next are belongingness and love needs, topped by esteem needs.

Esteem needs, including those for self-esteem, self-respect, and the esteem of others, are divided into two categories. The first category involves the way that we see ourselves, such as the desire for strength, achievement, mastery, independence, and freedom. The second category concerns the way others see us, including status, fame, dominance, recognition, and appreciation. Maslow describes the need for self-actualization when all of the lower level needs are met:

> Even if all these needs are satisfied, we may still often (if not always) expect that a new discontent and restlessness will soon develop, unless the individual is doing what he, individually, is fitted for. A musician must make music, an artist must paint, a poet must write, if he is to be ultimately at peace with himself. What a man can be, he must be. He must be true to his own nature. This need we may call self-actualization. . . .

It refers to a man's desire for self-fulfillment, namely, the tendency for him to become actualized in what he is potentially. This tendency might be phrased as the desire to become more and more what one idiosyncratically is, to become everything that one is capable of becoming.

The specific form that these needs will take of course varies greatly from person to person. In one person it may take the form of the desire to be an ideal mother, in another it may be expressed athletically, and in still another it may be expressed in painting pictures or in inventions.

Assertiveness

In *The Other Kind of Smart,* Harvey Deutschendorf notes: "Healthy assertive people, while being clear about their wishes, respect the rights of others. As much as assertive people maintain their boundaries, they respect the boundaries of others. Assertiveness allows for a difference of opinion without an attempt to beat the other person into submission or force them to come around to another way of thinking. It allows a win-win situation, something that aggression does not. It is possible for two quite assertive people to maintain a close friendship and respect one another while disagreeing with each other."

Relationships

According to Daniel Goleman in *Emotional Intelligence,* "Improving one's Emotional Intelligence involves, in handling relationships:

- Increased ability to analyze and understand relationships
- Better at resolving conflicts and negotiating agreements
- Better at solving problems in relationships
- More assertive and skilled at communicating
- More popular and outgoing, friendly and involved with peers
- More sought out by peers
- More concerned and considerate
- More pro-social and harmonious in groups

• More sharing, cooperation, and helpfulness
• More democratic in dealing with others"

Teamwork

Mel Silberman discusses teamwork in *People Smart:* "A person's ability to be interpersonally intelligent is really challenged when it comes to teamwork. All of us are involved in some kind of teamwork, whether at work, with another parent, in a neighborhood group, or in a service organization. Being part of a team is challenging because you have less personal control over the outcome than you might have in a one-on-one relationship. It's often frustrating because you have fewer opportunities to get your point across and persuade others. Working as a team takes special skills, such as complementing the styles of others, coordinating the efforts of team members without bossing them around, and building consensus."

PART II

INDIVIDUALS WHO WERE IN NEED OF PEOPLE SMARTS

Part II provides five role models from history that illustrate undervalued individuals who had accomplished significant things but who were unable to sell their ideas or inventions. Several of them ultimately met with success after much delay and frustration. For some of them, credit was never fully received for their achievements.

John Atanasoff, Inventor of the Computer

Robert Goddard, Rocketry Pioneer

Developers at Palo Alto Research Center, Xerox

Reginald Mitchell, Developer of the Spitfire

Chester Carlson, Inventor of Xerography

PART I

ROLE MODELS OF EMOTIONAL INTELLIGENCE

Perseverance	Social Responsibility
Empathy	Motivation
Optimism	Assertiveness
Persuasion / Negotiation	Relationships
Leadership	Teamwork
Emotional Control	

"The term 'Emotional Intelligence' is used to encompass an incisive, broad and diverse approach in describing closely related terms. Focus [is] on the following competencies:

- The ability to recognize and understand emotions and to express feelings non-destructively
- The ability to understand how others feel and relate with them cooperatively
- The ability to manage and control emotions effectively
- The ability to manage change and the emotions generated by change, and to adapt and solve problems of a personal and interpersonal nature
- The ability to generate positive affect and be self-motivated"

Reuven Bar-On, J. G. Maree, and Maurice Jesse Elias, eds., *Educating People to Be Emotionally Intelligent*

A purpose of Part I is to provide role models of Emotional Intelligence from history to illustrate the traits that make up the Emotional Quotient (EQ). According to author Samuel Smiles, "Example teaches better than precept. It is the best modeler of the character of men and women. To set a lofty example is the richest bequest a man [or woman] can leave behind."

All of these role models had a high EQ and a number of them are assumed to have had a high IQ as well. Also, they all had the Emotional Intelligence traits of perseverance, optimism, and motivation. In addition, since they were all achievers, they had other EQ traits that varied from individual to individual as well as additional positive traits, such as determination and resilience.

The examples provided are not an all-inclusive list of the traits of Emotional Intelligence. Others include independence, an aptitude for problem solving, and flexibility. We can learn from these role models to aid in increasing our own Emotional Intelligence.

CHAPTER 1

PERSEVERANCE—ROLE MODELS

Robert Bruce (1274-1329) King Robert I of Scotland

R. H. Macy (1822-1877) Founder of Macy's Department Store

"Nothing in the world can take the place of persistence.

Talent will not; nothing is more common than unsuccessful men with talent.

Genius will not; unrewarded genius is almost a proverb.

Education alone will not; the world is full of educated derelicts.

Persistence and determination alone are omnipotent."

Calvin Coolidge
(Appeared on the cover of the program for his memorial service in 1933)

ROBERT BRUCE—King Robert I of Scotland

"Whoever perseveres will be crowned."

Johann Gottfried Herder

In 1305 and early 1306, Scotland was ruled by Edward I of England, a strong, cruel Plantagenet king. Scotland had been a conquered country, or at least partly under English control, since 1296. The Scottish patriot, William Wallace, tried to throw off the English yoke with a rousing victory at Stirling Bridge in September 1297, but his forces lost the battle of Falkirk to the English longbow the following July and were reduced to guerrilla actions. Wallace was a commoner with no aspirations to the crown of Scotland.

In 1306, the two Scottish lords with the greatest claim to the throne were John Comyn of Badenoch, "the Red Comyn," who was the nephew of the previous king, John Balliol, and Robert Bruce, whose grandfather had been King of Scotland. John Comyn had been in communication with Edward I of England. When Robert Bruce heard of these discussions, he suggested that Comyn meet with him in the Church of the Minorite Friars in Dumfries.

The heirs to the throne argued heatedly near the high altar, and Robert Bruce fatally stabbed the Red Comyn. Bruce's companions claimed that it was self-defense. Bruce was concerned about losing the support of the Church by this act but was pardoned by the patriotic Bishop of Glasgow, Bishop Wishart. On Palm Sunday, 1306, Bruce was crowned Robert I, King of Scotland, at Scone.

Scotland was a divided country, and many Scottish lords sided with the English. Bruce's early encounters with the English and their Scottish allies were a series of defeats. In June 1306, he was routed at the battle of Methven in his first battle as King of Scotland. During the battle, Bruce was taken prisoner briefly but was rescued by his brother-in-law, Christopher Seton. Bishop Wishart was captured and imprisoned. Six of the knights who had supported Bruce at his coronation were captured, and sixteen nobles, including Christopher Seton, were hanged at Newcastle without a trial.

Bruce's rule was at an ebb, and many of his supporters were discouraged. He attempted to enlist men for his small army at Athol.

In August 1306, Bruce and his party camped on land belonging to John of Lorne, a distant Comyn relative. John of Lorne had heard that Bruce was in the area and had asked his tenants to watch for him and his men. Bruce's party was surprised by John of Lorne's men, and the King of Scotland was defeated again. Many of Bruce's party dispersed to avoid capture.

With a small following, Bruce "took to the heather," sleeping in caves and eating only a mixture of raw oatmeal and water, called drammock. After crossing Loch Lomond to Castle Donaverty, Bruce and his men traveled among the Islands of Kintyre and the Hebrides, participating in several forays and skirmishes along the way. They wintered on the Island of Rathlin off the coast of Ireland. The Irish natives didn't provide aid to the refugee Scots but, because they were also hostile to the English, didn't betray them to King Edward's forces.

According to a story passed down from generation to generation, the incident of the spider occurred at Rathlin. Bruce thought that his problems might be due to his killing the Red Comyn in the church at Dumfries, and he considered performing an act of contrition for this great sin. He thought about abandoning his quest to free Scotland from English rule to crusade in the Holy Land against the Saracens. However, he didn't want to shirk his duty as King of Scotland to free his country of the English invaders. He was torn between performing his duty to Scotland and atoning for his past sins. According to Sir Walter Scott in "History of Scotland" from *Tales of a Grandfather*:

> While he was divided twixt these reflections, and doubtful of what he would do, Bruce was looking upward toward the roof of the cabin in which he lay; and his eye was attracted by a spider which, hanging at the end of a long thread of its own spinning, was endeavoring, in the fashion of that creature, to swing itself from one beam in the roof to another, for the purpose of fixing the line on which it meant to stretch its web.

The insect made the attempt again and again without success, and at length Bruce counted that it had tried to carry its point six times, and been as often unable to do so. It came to his head that he had himself fought just six battles against the English and their allies and that the poor persevering spider was exactly in the same situation as himself, having made as many trials, and had been as often disappointed in what he had aimed at.

"Now," thought Bruce, "as I have no means of knowing what is best to be done, I shall be guided by the luck which guides this spider. If the spider shall make another effort to fix its thread and shall be successful, I will venture a seventh time to try my fortune in Scotland; but if the spider shall fail, I will go to the wars in Palestine, and never return to my home country more."

While Bruce was forming his resolution, the spider made another exertion with all the force it could muster, and fairly succeeded in fastening its thread to the beam which it had so often in vain attempted to reach. Bruce, seeing the success of the spider, resolved to try his own fortune; and as he had never before gained a victory, so he never afterward sustained any considerable or decisive check or defeat.

Bruce defeated the English decisively at Bannockburn in June 1314 and finally, in 1328, achieved his goal, the formal recognition of the independence of Scotland by the English Parliament.

R. H. MACY—Founder of Macy's Department Store

"Genius is only the power of making continuous efforts. The line between failure and success is so fine that we scarcely know when we pass it; so fine that we are often on the line but don't know it. How many a man has thrown up his hands at a time when a little more effort, a little more patience, would have achieved success. In business sometimes, prospects may seem darkest when they are really on the turn. A little more persistence, a little more effort, and what seemed hopeless failure may turn into glorious success. There is no failure except in no longer trying. There is no defeat except from within, no really insurmountable barrier save our own inherent weakness of purpose."

Elbert Hubbard

Rowland Hussey Macy was born on August 30, 1822, on Nantucket Island to John Macy and Eliza Myrick Macy, who were Quakers. John Macy, the captain of a sailing ship, was a descendent of Thomas Macy, the first white man to settle on the island. Many of the personal characteristics displayed by Macy in later years were nurtured in Nantucket, including drive, frugality, originality, and perseverance.

Macy's first job was crew member on the three-masted, 368-ton whaler, *Emily Morgan,* of New Bedford, Massachusetts. The ship stopped at Pernambuco, Brazil, sailed around Cape Horn, and put in at Samoa, the Gilbert Islands, Ascension Island, and New Zealand. On September 26, 1841, the *Emily Morgan* returned to New Bedford loaded with 3,000 barrels of sperm oil, over 100 barrels of whale oil, 1,000 pounds of whale bone, and a cask of ambergris, which was used in making perfume. Nineteen-year-old Macy returned home with his earnings for four years, one 175th share (about $500), which he used later to begin his first retail venture.

Macy moved to Boston and worked in several jobs, including an apprenticeship in a printing shop, before deciding to go into business for himself. In 1844, he opened his first retail store, a small thread and needle store at 78 1/2 Hanover Street in Boston. It failed in its first year. His second attempt in the retail business was a dry goods store at 357 Washington Street, Boston, in 1846. Macy sold mainly European-made items purchased at public auction.

This venture wasn't successful either, and he had to close this store in late 1847.

In 1848, Macy worked with his brother-in-law, Samuel S. Houghton, at a store located at 175 Tremont Street in Boston. Houghton, who later founded Houghton & Dutton, a Boston department store, specialized in embroidery and lace. Macy learned many of his principles of retailing from this early experience. He learned the advantages and disadvantages of doing business on credit and the value of intensive advertising. He learned from his failures.

Macy's next opportunity was in California during the gold rush. In 1849, Macy traveled to California with his brother Charles. In July 1850, Macy and his brother formed a partnership with two other men in Marysville, California, about forty miles north of Sacramento. Macy and Company sold clothing, other dry goods, and provisions.

Macy and Company competed with at least thirty other general stores in the area. Most of their customers were miners; when the gold ran out in the Marysville area, the miners moved on to the next find, and Macy and Company's business was reduced dramatically. In September 1850, they sold out, and Macy returned to Massachusetts with earnings of three to four thousand dollars. He had gained from this experience, since he had become familiar in dealing with customers from all over the world. He also learned about doing business on a large scale in an environment of inflated prices.

In April 1851, Macy began his fifth endeavor in the retail business, a dry goods store on Merrimack Street in the small town of Haverhill, Massachusetts. By this time, Macy was experienced in the retail business. Some of that experience was in what not to do.

Many of the ideas and operating methods that would serve him well in his New York store in later years were first implemented at the Haverhill store. He advocated the concept of selling at a fixed price (which wasn't common in the mid-nineteenth century), buying for cash, selling for cash, and advertising at about three times the rate of his competition.

Macy was his own advertising copywriter, and he was good at it. Not only was his advertising cleverly done, it was innovative, as in the use of considerable white space around his words to draw attention to them. Macy did most of the buying for his store personally. He bought from manufacturers and importers, not from wholesalers and jobbers. He eliminated one layer of middlemen.

However, Haverhill had too many dry goods stores to serve that small market. Macy went out of business just before Christmas, 1851. If imitation is the sincerest form of flattery, he should have been flattered. His competitors copied many of his techniques.

In November 1852, he reopened at a new location in Haverhill, in the New Granite Store at 68-74 Merrimack Street. He sold his goods for the lowest prices in town. However, by 1855, the combined population of Haverhill and nearby Bradford was just over 9,000, and the market he had chosen wasn't large enough to sustain a store. He sold out in July 1855.

In Macy's sixth failure in the retail business, he declared bankruptcy. He promised creditors fifty cents on the dollar, but he was able to pay only twenty-five cents. Macy salvaged two to three thousand dollars on which to live, but this black mark stayed on his credit record for ten years. He had to contend with it three years later when he founded his New York store.

Next, Macy became a stockbroker and exchange broker in Boston. In 1857, he moved to Superior City on Lake Superior in Wisconsin to work as a real estate broker and money broker. Heavy ship traffic was anticipated for the new Soo Locks, and substantial growth was predicted for Superior City. The financial panic of 1857 dashed that optimism. Macy returned to the East in 1858.

At this time, Macy was thirty-six years old and had been a whaler, retailer, gold miner, stockbroker, and real estate broker. He didn't have much to show for his efforts. A potential employer could look at his frequent job changes and not rate his prospects very high. However, that employer would've overlooked the overwhelming perseverance of the man. Macy also had good business sense; he knew value when he saw it, and he had considerable persuasive ability.

Macy used his persuasiveness in financing his next venture in the retail business, a small dry goods store at Sixth Avenue near 14th Street at Herald Square in Manhattan. The store, which was twenty feet wide and sixty feet deep, was financed by long-term credit from his suppliers. Considering his lack of cash and his previous track record, his success in obtaining credit was a tribute to his ability to sell himself.

Finally, Macy served a market in which he could be successful. New York had a total population of 950,000 in 1858, including

Brooklyn's 200,000 across the East River. New York was the largest city in the United States and was growing rapidly. Approximately two-thirds of U.S. imports came in through the Port of New York, and about one-third of exports left from there. New York was dominant in a number of areas, including banking, finance, clothing manufacturing, and wholesale dry goods.

Macy employed his established methods of operation and was successful beyond his dreams. He used the techniques that he had developed over the years, including selling for cash only, offering only one selling price, selling at low prices based on high volume, and using bold advertising. His offer of returning customers' money within a week if they were not satisfied with their purchase also contributed to his success.

A story told about the department store's relationship with its customers involved store manager Percy Straus, who promised one Christmas season that all purchases from Macy's would be delivered by Christmas day. Straus went to bed at midnight on Christmas Eve and was awakened at 2:00 a.m. by the sweet, feminine voice of a customer who told him that she was very satisfied with the dancing bear that she had bought for her granddaughter for Christmas. Straus said that he was happy to hear that, but asked why she called him at home at 2:00 a.m. to tell him. She explained that she was calling because his @#*&% truck had just awakened her delivering it.

Another story involved a regular Macy's customer who had ordered a flagpole to fly the Stars and Stripes on the Fourth of July. He had the flagpole installed in his front yard at his home in Connecticut, but it was shorter than the length he had ordered. He called Macy's, described his problem, and insisted that a flagpole the correct length be delivered. Macy's immediately sent a truck to Connecticut to deliver the second flagpole and to return the original one to the store. The customer had the second flagpole installed and found that this one was too long.

Frustrated, he went to a local store, bought one the desired length, and had this third pole installed on his lawn; he placed the pole from Macy's in his garage. He called Macy's to tell them to retrieve their flagpole and not to bother bringing a third one. The Macy's truck came on July 3 while the customer was out, dug up the flagpole from his front yard, and took it back to New York. The patriot from Connecticut flew the flag from the roof of his house that Fourth of July, but remained a loyal Macy's customer.

Macy credited much of the success of his New York store to Margaret Getchell LaForge, Macy's first woman executive. A distant relative of Macy's, Margaret Getchell started to work at the store as a cashier in late 1860. She advanced rapidly to a bookkeeping position and then to superintendent of the store. She was fair, tactful, and attentive to detail in supervising the day-to-day operations. She was known for her executive ability and was a strong influence on Macy in establishing policies for the operation of the store.

Getchell's motto was "Be Everywhere, Do Everything, and Never Forget to Astonish the Customer." She knew how to display items for sale and had a knack for publicity. She dressed two live cats in dolls' clothes and placed them in twin cribs in the toy department to attract customers. A sales clerk once dropped an expensive imported toy bird on the floor, breaking its singing mechanism. Getchell picked it up, removed a hairpin from her hair, and fixed it on the spot. She was a take-charge person.

In 1869, Getchell married Abiel T. LaForge, Macy's lace buyer and a trusted employee, who had been a fellow Union officer of Macy's son in the Civil War. LaForge became a partner of R. H. Macy & Company in 1872; Robert Macy Valentine, Macy's nephew, became a partner in 1875.

On March 29, 1877, Rowland Hussey Macy died while on a buying trip to Paris. Abiel LaForge and Valentine managed the store, but within a brief time LaForge died of tuberculosis contracted during the war. Shortly afterward, both Mrs. LaForge and Valentine died. Charles B. Webster, a former floorwalker who had been made a partner after the death of Macy and LaForge, became store manager.

In 1887, Webster approached Isador and Nathan Straus, sellers of imported china and glassware in rented space at Macy's since 1874, with an invitation to become partners. In 1898, Webster sold his interest in the store to the Straus family. More than five generations of the Straus family have been involved with the store.

Without perseverance, Macy would have been an unknown. By persevering, His efforts resulted in the largest store in the world under one roof, with 2,200,000 square feet spread over an entire city block. The department store is known for producing the Macy's Thanksgiving Day Parade and as the location for the original version of the movie, *Miracle on 34th Street*. To many people, Macy's is an institution.

* * *

Robert Bruce and R. H. Macy were perseverers. Bruce was also strong in leadership and motivation. Fortunately, he hung on and earned the throne that was rightfully his. It is notable that he overcame six straight losses in battle.

Macy was strong in persuasion / negotiation with his suppliers and in relationships with his employees as well. He was also creative in eliminating the middleman of his suppliers and in introducing installment buying. He had the resilience to bounce back from six losing store locations before moving to Herald Square in New York City.

CHAPTER 2

EMPATHY—ROLE MODELS

Louis Pasteur (1822-1895) Pioneer in Medical Science

Albert Schweitzer (1875-1965) Author and Physician in Africa

"The ability to see the world from another person's perspective, the capacity to tune into what someone else might be thinking and feeling about a situation, regardless of how that view might differ from your own perception, is an extremely strong interpersonal tool. When you make an empathetic statement, even in the midst of an otherwise tense or antagonistic encounter, you shift the balance. A contentious and uneasy interchange becomes a more collaborative alliance."

Steven J. Stein and Howard E. Book, *The EQ Edge*

LOUIS PASTEUR—Pioneer in Medical Science

"These three things—work, will, success—fill human existences. Will opens the door to success, both brilliant and happy. Work passes through these doors, and at the other end of the journey success comes in to crown one's efforts."

Louis Pasteur

Pasteur is known for his work with the process of fermentation and for the development of pasteurization, which has saved many lives over the years. He is also known for his knowledge of diseases that attack the human body and of the means by which the body can be protected from those diseases or be treated for them.

Pasteur, a great scientist, was known as a crusader for human welfare as well as a seeker of scientific truth. He advocated his ideas in public debates before those ideas were generally accepted. As with many people on the leading edge of change, he was vilified and accused of misleading the public.

Louis Pasteur was born on December 27, 1822, in Dôle near Dijon in the Jura region of France and grew up in nearby Arbois. His father, Jean Joseph Pasteur, had fought in Napoleon's army in the Peninsular War.

In elementary school, Pasteur was not a particularly serious student. In his teens, he developed a strong interest in painting. He was considered talented by other artists and, to his parents' dismay, thought that he might become a painter.

At sixteen, Pasteur enrolled in the Lycée St. Louis, a secondary school in Paris, and four years later attended lectures at the Sorbonne, where he was impressed by the chemistry lectures. He received a Bachelor of Science degree from the Royal College of Besançon; his studies in chemistry were considered "barely adequate."

However, in 1847, Pasteur finished his dissertation on crystallography and earned a doctorate from the École Normale Supérieure in Paris. He accepted a position as professor of physics at Dijon before becoming professor of chemistry at Strasbourg University.

Pasteur fell in love with Marie Laurent, daughter of the rector of Strasbourg University, and proposed two weeks after meeting her. They were married on May 29, 1848. The story circulated that Pasteur was late for his wedding because he wanted to complete the experiment on which he was working. Marie was the ideal wife for Pasteur. Their friend and Pasteur's colleague, Émile Roux, described their relationship:

> From the first days of their common life, Madame Pasteur understood what kind of man she had married; she did everything to protect him from the difficulties of life, taking onto herself the worries of the home, that he might retain the full freedom of his mind for his investigations. Madame Pasteur loved her husband to the extent of understanding his studies. During the evenings she wrote dictation, calling for explanations, for she took a genuine interest in crystalline structure or in attenuated viruses. Madame was more than an incomparable companion, she was his best collaborator.

In 1854, Pasteur joined the faculty of sciences at the University of Lille and began the study that established his reputation. Naturalists, from the beginning of recorded history, believed in "spontaneous generation"—that living matter could be produced from dead substances. Pasteur conducted a series of controlled experiments to prove that only a living thing could produce life. Other scientists mocked and scorned him, refusing to believe that microbes could cause fermentation. Pasteur observed, "A man of science may hope for what may be said of him in the future, but he cannot stop to think of the insults—or the compliments—of his own day."

Pasteur was asked to save the silk industry in France. Silkworms had been infected with a disease that was destroying the industry. He interviewed silkworm cultivators in Alès and collected eggs, larvae, and moths. When he failed to suggest a quick solution, he was treated harshly and called a "mere chemist." When he suggested that diseased eggs be culled out to protect the healthy ones, his character was attacked. During a four-year period, however, he diagnosed the problem and ended the epidemic.

In 1859, Pasteur's oldest daughter, Jeanne, died of typhus. In 1865, his youngest child, Camille, died of a fever, and his twelve-year-old daughter, Cécile, died of typhoid fever the following year. The overworked Pasteur reeled from these multiple shocks and was temporarily paralyzed. His speech and his left arm and leg were affected by a cerebral hemorrhage.

Pasteur returned to work against the advice of his doctors. In *Pasteur and Modern Science,* René Dubos commented on his determination: "This performance revealed once more that Pasteur was a man of indomitable will. It was not only his opponents that he wanted to overpower; it was also nature—it was himself."

Pasteur studied the microorganisms that spoiled wine and beer. He developed the process of partial sterilization, which became known as pasteurization, by heating a liquid to fifty to sixty degrees Centigrade. He applied the process to many beverages including beer, cider, milk, and wine. Although he designed much of the equipment used in pasteurization, he chose not to profit from these developments.

In 1877, Pasteur began his work on anthrax. Earlier, with studies on potato blight in 1850 and silkworms in 1868, it had been shown that microbes could cause disease. Studies on anthrax showed, for the first time, that microbes caused diseases affecting higher animals and human beings. Robert Koch, the noted German bacteriologist, worked during the same period of time as Pasteur. Pasteur and Koch are considered the co-founders of the field of microbiology. Koch determined the life cycle of the anthrax bacillus and developed culture methods to determine the microbes that caused tuberculosis and cholera.

In the Auvergne district of France, from thirty to fifty percent of the sheep population had died from anthrax. Pasteur isolated the bacteria that causes anthrax and used the bacteria to cure the disease. Doctors and ministers attacked Pasteur's germ theory. In *Makers of the Modern World,* Louis Untermeyer observed:

> Nevertheless, Pasteur persisted. He surmised that a bacterial attack induced a formation in the blood of "antibodies" which attacked the germs; in fatal diseases, the invading germs multiplied so quickly as to cause death before enough antibodies could

form. He experimented with the deadly, filament-shaped bacteria and subjected them to endless tests and counter-tests. Finally, he devised a culture which was a mild form of the disease itself and, instead of killing, would build up a protection against the fever.

Pasteur's success with anthrax finally brought him the recognition that he deserved. He was awarded the Legion of Honor by the government of France and was admitted to the French Academy.

Pasteur's next effort was to isolate the bacteria that caused rabies and to develop a vaccine. In July 1885, a nine-year-old boy from Alsace who had been bitten fourteen times on the hands, legs, and thighs by a rabid dog was brought to Pasteur. Pasteur's treatment had only been used on dogs, not on humans. He was not sure how strong to make the serum or what the side effects, if any, would be. However the boy was deathly ill and would not live unless Pasteur could save his life. Pasteur increased the dosage slowly, and the boy's life was saved.

On November 14, 1887, the Pasteur Institute, a laboratory for biological research, opened. It owed its existence to contributions from many countries, as well as gifts from wealthy sponsors and many donations from the working class. Five years later, scientists gathered at the Sorbonne to honor Pasteur. Joseph Lister, representing the Royal Societies of England and Scotland, was one of many speakers. He said to Pasteur, "You have raised the veil which for centuries had covered infectious diseases. You have changed the treatment of wounds from an uncertain and too often disastrous business into a scientific and certainly beneficial art. Your relentless researches have thrown a powerful light which has illuminated the dark places in surgery."

In 1889, Pasteur suffered a serious attack of uremic poisoning and almost died. He wanted to return to the laboratory but realized that he did not have the strength to go back to work. When he was seventy-three, his health declined rapidly; he became too weak to raise his head, and he had difficulty speaking. He lapsed into a coma and died on September 28, 1895.

Pasteur was widely quoted for insights such as "change favors only the mind which is prepared." One of his most profound observations is:

> Two contrary laws seem to be wrestling for the soul of man. The one is the law of blood and death, always planning new methods of destruction, forcing nations to be constantly ready for the battlefield. The other is a law of peace, work, and health, always creating new means of delivering man from the scourges which beset him. The one seeks violent conquests; the other the relief of humanity. Which of the two will ultimately prevail, God alone knows. But we may assert that science will have tried, by obeying the law of humanity, to extend the frontiers of life.

Several years after Pasteur's death, a poll was taken in France to determine which of their countrymen they considered the greatest heroes. Napoleon was ranked fifth; Pasteur was first. In *The 100: A Ranking of the Most Influential Persons in History* by Michael H. Hart, Pasteur is ranked twelfth, before other scientists: Charles Darwin (seventeenth), Michael Faraday (twenty-eighth), James Clerk Maxwell (twenty-ninth), and Alexander Fleming (forty-fifth). He also ranked ahead of Aristotle, Moses, Augustus Caesar, Genghis Khan, Martin Luther, Constantine the Great, and George Washington.

In *How Pasteur Changed History: The Story of Louis Pasteur and the Pasteur Institute,* Moira Davison Reynolds commented on Pasteur's personal characteristics: "He made excellent deductions about the information at hand; and, blessed with keen observation and superb intuition, he designed and executed reproducible experiments that would prove or disprove his hypotheses. In addition to his intellectual gifts, Pasteur would exhibit emotional qualities that were to his advantage. He was enthusiastic about whatever he was working on, and unsatisfactory or disappointing results did not seriously daunt him. He had patience. He also possessed a fighting spirit and the capacity to work untiringly." In his work, he certainly displayed empathy and his feelings for others.

ALBERT SCHWEITZER—Author and Physician in Africa

"What to my friends seemed almost irrational in my plan was that I wanted to go to Africa, not as a missionary, but as a doctor. Already thirty years of age, I would burden myself with long and laborious study. I wanted to be a doctor so that I might be able to work without being able to talk. For years, I had been giving of myself in words, and it was with joy that I followed the calling of theological teacher and preacher. But this new form of activity would consist not in preaching the religion of love, but in practicing it. Medical knowledge would make it possible for me to carry out my intentions in the best and most complete way, wherever the path of service might lead me."

Albert Schweitzer

Albert Schweitzer was born on January 14, 1875, in Kaysersberg, Alsace. Schweitzer's father, Louis, was pastor of the Lutheran church. After the Thirty Years War, Alsace had become part of Germany.

As a young man, Schweitzer studied piano and organ. His music teacher was Eugene Munch, whose nephew Charles was to become the conductor of the Boston Symphony Orchestra. Bach and Wagner were two of young Schweitzer's favorite composers. He did well in school, but he was not at the top of his class. As a youth, he observed that experience resulted in decision, and decision resulted in action.

Schweitzer attended college at Strasbourg. He studied philosophy and religion and was very serious about his religious studies. He searched for knowledge of the Bible and knowledge of his fellow man. He continued on for a doctorate. The subject of his doctoral dissertation was the religious philosophy of Kant.

At the age of twenty-one, Schweitzer determined what he was going to do with his life: "It struck me as inconceivable that I should be allowed to lead such a happy life while I saw so many people around me struggling with sorrow and suffering. Even at school I had felt stirred whenever I caught a glimpse of the miserable home surroundings of some of my classmates. I could not help but think continually of others who were denied good fortune by their material circumstances or their health."

Schweitzer decided "that I could consider myself justified in living till I was thirty devoting myself to scholarship arts, but after that I would devote myself directly to serving humanity. I had already tried many times to to find the meaning that lay hidden in the saying of Jesus: 'Whosoever would save his life shall lose it, and whosoever shall lose his life for My sake and the Gospel's shall save it.' Now I had found the answer. I could now add outward to inward happiness.'"

Next Schweitzer had to determine what form his service to humanity would take. A magazine had been placed on his work table containing the article, "The Needs of the Congo Mission" by Alfred Boegner, president of the Paris Missionary Society, who noted that the mission did not have sufficient people to do its work in Gabon, the northern province of the Congo. Boegner hoped that his appeal would bring forward someone "on whom the Master's eyes already rested" to offer their services. The author observed: "Men and women who can reply simply to the Master's call, 'Lord, I am coming,' those are the people the Church needs." Schweitzer's search was over; he had found what his service to humanity would be. He wanted a "hands-on" career, not an administrative one.

In October 1905, Schweitzer told his unsuspecting family and friends that "at the beginning of the winter term I should enter myself as a medical student, in order to go later to Equatorial Africa as a doctor." The university was surprised, as were his friends, that he would undertake a different curriculum at the age of thirty; nevertheless, he was accepted into medical school. In addition to his medical studies, he continued with his interest in the physical sciences and the organ, as well as organ building. His final medical examination in May 1908 consisted of the subjects of anatomy, physiology, and the natural sciences. Strasbourg did not offer study in tropical medicine; he had to go to Paris for that as well as to obtain medical supplies for the tropics.

Schweitzer received support for his move to Africa from the Missionary Society in Paris, but not the financial support he needed. He knocked on doors of wealthy friends and acquaintances asking for contributions.

Helene Breslau, Schweitzer's assistant who had helped him with his books, correspondence, and even his organ practice, was determined to go to Africa with him. They had known each other for nine years and decided to get married, which they did on June 18, 1912.

Schweitzer and Helene sailed for Africa from Bordeaux on the steamship *Europe*. Dakar was their first port on African soil. From there, they sailed to Libreville, Gabon, and onward to Cape Lopez at the mouth of the Ogowe and then to Lambarene, over 100 miles from the coast. In the local dialect, Lambarene means "let us try." The mission station in Lambarene had been established in 1876 by Dr. Nassau, an American medical man and missionary.

To house his medical practice, Schweitzer had been promised a wooden bungalow on rows of iron pilings to allow for runoff after the rains. Unfortunately, it hadn't been built. He had to use an old chicken coop as his consulting room.

In their small bungalow, the Schweitzers had to adjust to a houseful of spiders and cockroaches. At six a.m. on the first morning, the line of patients formed. He was not to get the time to get settled that he had requested. Most of his equipment and drugs were over one hundred miles away on the coast. The assistant and interpreter that he had arranged for was not there either due to a legal dispute, a frequent occurrence in Africa.

Schweitzer had not expected for the sick to be so numerous or to include so many who suffered from multiple ailments. The most common were "skin diseases of various sorts, malaria, sleeping sickness, leprosy, elephantiasis, heart complaints, suppurating injuries to the bones (osteomyelitis), and tropical dysentery." Poor diet contributed to the ill-health of the natives. People lived on manioc, yams, and bananas.

By late autumn, Schweitzer moved his practice into a corrugated-iron building twenty-six feet long and thirteen feet wide containing three rooms: a consulting room, an operating room, and small dispensary. Large bamboo huts were constructed around this building for the patients. Helene, who had trained as a nurse, assisted in the hospital.

After a few months, the hospital treated forty patients a day; accommodations had to be provided for those who came with them to Lambarene. Schweitzer and Helene treated almost 2,000 patients in their first nine months in addition to their building effort. Schweitzer worked long days. Eventually, other doctors assisted Schweitzer with the workload, allowing him time to write.

The first visit to Africa was from 1913-1917. The Schweitzers returned to Europe, which was good for Helene, whose health was not strong. Schweitzer served as a physician and preacher in Strasbourg.

The Schweitzers' second period in Africa was from 1924-1927. The hospital buildings at Lambarene had been allowed to fall into disrepair. Considerable work was required to raise collapsed buildings and to clear the overgrown grounds. A dysentery epidemic made it necessary to move the hospital to a larger site, one not surrounded by water, swamp, and steep hills. In January 1927, patients moved into the new hospital.

In 1927, the Schweitzers returned to Europe, where he occupied himself with lecturing and fund-raising. He said, "People often ask me, why did you go to Africa? Because my Master told me to."

Schweitzer's third residence in Africa was from 1928-1932. Over his lifetime, Schweitzer, spent thirteen sojourns in Africa, alternating with visits to Europe, where he received many honorary degrees. Most of his writing was done on his trips back to Europe.

In October 1953, Schweitzer was awarded the Nobel Peace Prize. He celebrated his ninetieth birthday on January 14, 1965, and died on September 4 in Lambarene.

In *Dr. Schweitzer of Lambarene,* Norman Cousins noted:

> The greatness of Schweitzer—indeed the essence of Schweitzer—is the man as symbol. It is not so much what he has done for others, but what others have done because of him and the power of his example. This is the measure of the man. What has come out of his life and thought is the kind of inspiration that can animate a generation. He has supplied a working demonstration of reverence for life. He represents enduring proof that we need not torment ourselves about the nature of human purpose. The scholar, he once wrote, must not live for science alone, nor the businessman for his business, nor the artist for his art. If affirmation of life is genuine, it will "demand for all that they should sacrifice a portion of their own life for others."

* * *

Louis Pasteur and Albert Schweitzer, excellent examples of the trait of empathy, could see things from the viewpoint of other people. They certainly had concern for others and helped others: Pasteur by providing additional medical treatments and Schweitzer by providing medical care to those who would not have received it otherwise.

Pasteur's early experiments were ridiculed by other scientists, but he continued with his work because he knew that he was on the right path. Schweitzer's relatives and friends were amazed when he decided to go to medical school so he could go to Africa to provide medical care for the natives. He recognized the value of individual accomplishments such as his writing and preaching, but he wanted to do something for others.

CHAPTER 3

OPTIMISM—ROLE MODELS

Paul Wittgenstein (1897-1961) One-armed Concert Pianist

Stephen Hawking (1942-   ) Researcher of Black Holes

"Optimism is the ability to see hope and stay positive in all situations and times, regardless of how bleak the present may be. When things are going well, it is quite easy to be upbeat and in good spirits. Success, however, demands that we be able to see hope and possibility even after major setbacks. One of the common denominators of successful people is their ability to bounce back after failures."

Harvey Deutschendorf, *The Other Kind of Smart*

PAUL WITTGENSTEIN—One-armed Concert Pianist

"It [learning to play the piano with one hand] was like attempting to scale a mountain. If you can't climb up from one side, you try another."

Paul Wittgenstein

Paul Wittgenstein was a highly regarded concert pianist prior to World War I. While serving in the Austrian army, he was severely wounded in the right arm, which had to be amputated. For most musicians, loss of an arm would have been a career-ending event. Wittgenstein, however, surveyed the music that could be played with one hand and practiced seven hours a day to learn how to play it.

In *The Music Review*, E. Fred Flindell commented on this accomplishment:

> Wittgenstein amazed the post-war generation. In the years following the war, a period of bizarre turmoil and stunting cynicism, Wittgenstein not only attained world-wide fame, his example fostered a unique image in the minds of scholars, concert-goers, and musicians alike. Neither his family, his wealth, his heroic war record, nor his musical talent could alone account for or carve out such an achievement. His was simply a boundless idealism, one embodying devotion, endurance, and temerity in the service of music.

Paul Wittgenstein, who was born on November 5, 1897, in Vienna, Austria, was the seventh of eight children of Karl and Leopoldine Kalmus Wittgenstein. Karl owned several steel factories and became known as the "Iron King" of Austria. Leopoldine Wittgenstein, the daughter of a wealthy merchant, played arrangements for four hands on the organ and piano with young Paul as his skill on the keyboard developed. Paul's younger brother, Ludwig, became a renowned philosopher.

The Wittgenstein family was wealthy. They frequently entertained Brahms, Mahler, and Clara Schumann. Paul was fortunate to have the opportunity to play piano duets with Richard Strauss. Bruno Walter and Pablo Casals also performed in the Wittgenstein home. Karl Wittgenstein provided financial support to Arnold Schöenberg.

Young Wittgenstein took piano lessons from the highly regarded teacher, Malvine Brée. Wittgenstein had an incredible memory for music and was a facile sight-reader. His exposure to masters of music in his home elevated his interest in music. He was not concerned about his own limitations in comparison with them. Next he took lessons from Theodor Leschetizky and the blind Austrian composer, Josef Labor. They helped him search for his own musical identity.

Wittgenstein's friend, Trevor Harvey, said about him at this time, "By all accounts in his early days he built up an astonishing left-hand technique, but when I knew him the nervous intensity that he developed led him often to play insensitively and loudly, and not always with great accuracy." He referred to himself as the "Saitenknicker," the mighty key smasher.

In December 1913, Wittgenstein made his debut as a concert pianist at the Grosser Musikverein Saal in Vienna. Three months later, he gave a solo performance with the Vienna Symphony Verein. In August 1914, he was called to active duty as a second lieutenant in the Austrian Army. He was severely wounded while leading a reconnaissance patrol near Zamosc, Poland.

In his book about Wittgenstein, *The Crown Prince*, John Barchilon described what happened when Wittgenstein's patrol was hit by an artillery shell:

> The ground opened up and hurled them in the air, spinning and twisting. Paul saw earth, fire, and sky. Arms, legs, and black dirt swirled around him, and then he began the endless journey back to earth. He fell and fell and fell, landing on something soft. Where were his legs? His arms, hands, where were they? Where was his foot? He heard nothing. Just silence. Black, black nothing. Was this death?

Wittgenstein was taken to an army hospital at Krasnostov, where his right arm was amputated. He was taken prisoner by the Russian Army at the hospital and moved to hospitals in Minsk and in Orel and Omsk, Siberia, where he had access to a piano. In November 1915, through efforts of the International Red Cross, he was sent from Siberia to Sweden, where he participated in a prisoner exchange sponsored by the Pope.

In March 1916, Wittgenstein was promoted to first lieutenant and retired on a medical disability pension. Leopoldine Wittgenstein received a letter from his commanding officer:

> I wish to express my sincere sympathy with you in connection with the severe wounding of your son. You may be proud of him, because owing to the information obtained by his patrol, the efforts of the Russians to attack us at Famorz were frustrated. He has rendered outstanding services, and I sincerely hope he will get official recognition.

In May 1916, Wittgenstein was awarded the Military Cross Class III and the War Decoration Class III. Five months later, he was awarded the Military Cross Class II by the Grand Duke of Mecklenburg. From the summer of 1917 until August 1918, by his own request, he served as a first lieutenant on the Italian front as a general's aide.

From the time of his return to Vienna until he volunteered for the Italian front, Wittgenstein practiced compositions for the left hand. He performed in five recitals, in which he played Labor's *Concertpiece for Piano and Orchestra, Sonata in E Flat for Piano and Violin,* and *Piano Quartet in C minor.* In September 1918, he returned to Vienna and the concert stage.

Leschetizky had died in 1915. Wittgenstein did not look for another teacher; he practiced seven hours a day, establishing his own regimen. Initially, he tired easily and had to rest frequently. From 1918 to 1921, Wittgenstein searched libraries, museums, and second-hand retail music shops for compositions for the left hand. He liked Brahms's arrangement of Bach's *Chaconne,* as well as Godowsky's *Suite for the Left Hand Alone,* the *Fugue upon Bach,* and the *Intermezzo and Etude Macabre.* He also admired *Studies for the Left Hand* by Reger, *Etudes for the Left Hand* by Saint-Saëns, and Scriabin's *Prelude and Nocturne for the Left Hand,* which the composer wrote after developing tendonitis in his right hand.

One of the earliest one-armed pianists was the Hungarian Count Geza Zichy, who began playing the piano at the age of five; he decided to be a concert pianist after losing his right arm in a hunting accident in 1864, when he was fifteen. His concert in Berlin in May 1915 was the first known public performance of a one-armed pianist. Count Zichy's friend, Franz Liszt, transcribed a song for him, and Emil Sauer wrote *Etude* for him. Wittgenstein did not like the works that Count Zichy composed for himself.

Wittgenstein wrote his own arrangements of piano compositions and operas using the transcription devices of Liszt and of Godowsky. He also commissioned composers to create new works for the left hand. Wittgenstein observed: "Since it is no particular attainment of mine, I think I may honestly say that I am (perhaps) the pianist for whom the greatest number of special compositions have been written." In 1931, he accepted a teaching position at the New Vienna Conservatory, where he was known for his energy and his optimism.

Wittgenstein didn't hesitate to make extensive changes to other composers' works that he had commissioned, similar to his modifications to Brahms's transcription of Bach's *Chaconne*. He made changes to the compositions of Hindemith and Korngold, as well as to Britten's *Diversions on a Theme*, Prokofiev's *Concerto No. 4*, and *Parergon to the Domestic Symphony* by Richard Strauss. They were twentieth-century composers, and Wittgenstein's style was that of the nineteenth century.

Wittgenstein asked Ravel if he would compose a piano concerto for the left hand. He willingly undertook the project. Initially, Ravel and Wittgenstein did not agree on the finished work. Wittgenstein objected to Ravel's inclusion of jazz rhythms in his composition; however, the differences were resolved. Ravel's *Concerto in D for Left Hand* became one of the most frequently played works for one hand.

Wittgenstein continued to perform on the concert stage. One of his students in the 1930s recalled the first time she had heard him play: "I was about twelve years old when I heard Paul Wittgenstein perform for the first time. I was sitting with my father in our subscription seats in the rear of the Weiner Musikverein Saal. After the concert, my father asked me if I had noticed anything unusual about the pianist. I had not. He told me that the pianist had only played with his left hand. I could not believe it."

In November 1934, Wittgenstein performed the Ravel *Concerto for the Left Hand and Orchestra* with the Boston Symphony. The music critic of the New York *Herald-Tribune* reported:

> Doubtless the greatest tribute one could pay to Paul Wittgenstein, the famous one-armed pianist, is a simple statement of the fact that after the first few moments wondering how the devil he accomplished it, one almost forgot that one was listening to a player whose right sleeve hung empty at his side. One found oneself engrossed by the sensitiveness of the artist's phrasing, the extent to which his incredible technique was subordinated to the delivery of the musical thought.

Wittgenstein taught at the New Vienna Conservatory until he immigrated to the United States in December 1938. From 1938 until 1943, he taught at the Ralph Wolfe Conservatory in New Rochelle, an affiliate of the Mannes Music School; from 1940 until 1945 he was a professor of piano at Manhattanville College of the Sacred Heart. He became a U.S. citizen in 1946. In 1957, Wittgenstein published *School for the Left Hand.* In 1958, he received an honorary Doctor of Music degree from the Philadelphia Musical Academy.

In a June 1967 interview with Leonard Castle, Wittgenstein described some of the piano technique that he used in concerts. He did not use the middle or harp pedal on the piano. He used two fingers on one key for increased volume, and difficult leaps over the keys could be avoided by half pedaling that simulated the two-handed technique. His skill was enhanced by the speed with which he used his left hand and his precise control.

On March 3, 1961, Paul Wittgenstein died in Manhasset, New York. In *The Music Review*, E. Fred Flindell wrote what might be considered an epitaph:

> It is, however, astonishing how many works [over forty] the artist took an active part in commissioning, determining, and performing. Few knew that Wittgenstein spent years helping others as president of the Society Against Poverty, or of his countless anonymous and gracious deeds of assistance. Perhaps his nineteenth-century ideas and bearing were at times anachronistic, even quixotic. Still, his endeavor and influence, his courage and skill will remain legendary for generations to come.

STEPHEN HAWKING —Researcher of "Black Holes"

"It is the most persistent and greatest adventure in human history, this search to understand the universe, how it works and where it came from. It is difficult to imagine that a handful of residents of a small planet circulating an insignificant star in a small galaxy have as their aim a complete understanding of the entire universe, a small speck of creation truly believing it is capable of understanding the whole."

Murray Gell-Mann

As an undergraduate, Stephen Hawking was an undistinguished student. He was not highly motivated; he studied an average of one hour a day. In 1963, at the age of twenty-one, Hawking was told that he had amyotrophic lateral sclerosis (ALS), which is known as motor neuron disease in Britain and Lou Gehrig's disease in the United States. ALS attacks the nerves of the spinal cord and the portion of the brain that controls voluntary motor functions of the muscles. The nerve cells degenerate, causing muscles to atrophy throughout the body, resulting in paralysis. Memory and the ability to think are not affected.

ALS, which worsens in stages, forces the patient to deal with a series of progressively limiting plateaus. Hawking has made incredible contributions to science by ignoring his ailment, to the extent of his ability. He has probably done more than any scientist to expand our understanding of the origin and nature of the universe, and his theoretical work on "black holes" was innovative. He is especially well known for one of his books, *A Brief History of Time*, a best seller.

Stephen Hawking was born in Oxford, England, on January 8, 1942, the three-hundredth anniversary of the death of the Italian scientist, Galileo. Both of Hawking's parents, Frank and Isobel Hawking, had attended Oxford University. Hawking wanted to major in either physics or mathematics in college, but his father insisted that his son take chemistry so that he could follow him in a medical career.

Hawking won a scholarship to University College, Oxford University. When he completed his undergraduate studies at Oxford, he took the final examinations upon which admission to graduate school were based. Hawking needed a first-class honors degree to be admitted to graduate school at Cambridge University to study cosmology with Dr. Fred Hoyle, the foremost British astronomer of his time. In October 1962, when Hawking began his graduate studies at Cambridge, he could choose between two areas of research, elementary particles—the study of small particles, or cosmology—the study of large objects. Cosmology is the study of the origin, evolution, and destiny of the universe.

In Hawking's opinion, "I thought that elementary particles were less attractive, because, although they were finding lots of new particles, there was no proper theory of elementary particles. All they could do was arrange the particles in families, like in botany. In cosmology, on the other hand, there was a well-defined theory—Einstein's general theory of relativity."

Instead of studying with Fred Hoyle, Hawking was assigned to Dennis Sciama, an unknown to him. He was discouraged by this until he realized that Hoyle, who traveled abroad frequently, would not have been as good a mentor as Sciama, a respected scientist who conscientiously guided him in his research.

Hawking also had a personal problem with which to contend. He began to have difficulty tying his shoelaces, he bumped into walls and furniture, and, on a few occasions, he fell. Also, he experienced slurred speech without having a drink to blame it on. When he arrived home for Christmas vacation, his parents, who hadn't seen him for several months, knew immediately that something was wrong. His father thought that he might have contracted a disease in the Middle East during a trip with him over the summer. His parents referred him to a specialist.

At several parties over the holidays, Hawking met and talked with Jane Wilde, the friend of a friend, who attended the local high school. Jane planned to read modern languages at Westfield College in London in the fall. She was attracted to this intellectual and somewhat eccentric character. Their relationship bloomed from their first meeting.

In January, Hawking underwent a battery of tests; the diagnosis was ALS. He faced decreasing mobility, gradual paralysis, and ultimately death as respiratory muscles lost their functionality or he contracted pneumonia. Many ALS patients do not live two years beyond the diagnosis.

If Hawking had decided to study experimental physics instead of theoretical physics, his career would have been over. He went into a deep depression, locked himself in his room, and listened to music, particularly his favorite composer, Wagner.

Hawking questioned continuing with his research, because he might not be around long enough to get his Ph.D. Literally, he felt that he had nothing to live for. He was not a deeply religious person; nevertheless, he had an experience that helped to put things into perspective: "While I was in hospital, I had seen a boy I vaguely knew die of leukemia in the bed opposite me. It had not been a pretty sight. Clearly there were people who were worse off than me. At least my condition didn't make me feel sick. Whenever I feel inclined to feel sorry for myself, I remember that boy."

Jane visited Stephen early in his stay in the hospital and was surprised to find that he had lost the will to live. Their relationship strengthened; she was a major factor in Hawking's turning his life around. His interest in his research was revived.

During his first two years at Cambridge, Hawking's physical condition worsened. He had to use a cane, and, occasionally, he fell. He rejected offers of help in getting around. His speech grew increasingly difficult to understand. He and Jane became engaged. She said, "I wanted to find some purpose to my existence, and I suppose I found it in the idea of looking after him. But we were in love." For Hawking, their engagement gave new direction to his life and gave him something to live for.

Hawking met applied mathematician Roger Penrose at a series of scientific meetings at Kings College in London. Penrose explained his concept of a singularity—a mass with zero size and infinite density—occurring at the center of a black hole, a region in space where gravity is so strong that not even light can escape. He showed that the collapse of a star could lead to the formation of a singularity. One night on the train back to Cambridge from London, Hawking turned to Dennis Sciama and speculated what would happen if Penrose's singularity theory were applied to the entire universe.

Penrose had showed that the collapse of a star could cause the formation of a singularity. Hawking conjectured that an important event had begun with the singularity. The event was the reverse of Penrose's collapse, an outward explosion named by Fred Hoyle the "big bang," the origin of the universe. The "big bang" is considered to be the tremendous explosion that began the expansion of the universe fifteen billion years ago.

When Hawking applied Penrose's ideas to the entire universe, he really began to devote himself to his work: "I started working hard for the first time in my life. To my surprise, I found I liked it. Maybe it is not really fair to call it work. Someone once said, 'Scientists get paid for doing what they enjoy.'" This effort became the final chapter of Hawking's dissertation, "Properties of the Expanding Universe," the work for which he was awarded a Ph.D by Cambridge University. Hawking looked for a post with a salary so that he and Jane could get married. He applied for a theoretical physics fellowship at Caius College, Cambridge University. He was awarded the fellowship, and he and Jane were married in July 1965.

Hawking's condition continued to decline. He now needed crutches to walk, and his ability to speak worsened. He had a difficult time getting around their house, but he refused offers of help. His strong-willed nature presented a challenge for Jane. She said, "Some would call his attitude determination, some obstinacy. I've called it both at one time or another. I suppose that's what keeps him going."

When asked whether he ever became depressed over his condition, Hawking replied, "Not normally, I have managed to do what I wanted to do despite it, and that gives a feeling of achievement." He maintained a positive outlook, and he was generally cheerful. He didn't waste time worrying about his health.

Hawking's approach to his work was largely intuitive—he had a feel for the correctness of an idea. He described his modus operandi:

> I work very much on intuition, thinking that, well, a certain idea ought to be right. Then I try to prove it. Sometimes I find I'm wrong. Sometimes I find that the original idea was wrong, but that leads to new ideas. I find it a great help to discuss my ideas with other people. Even if they don't contribute anything, just having to explain it to someone else helps me sort it out for myself.

At the end of the 1960s, Jane and their friends convinced Hawking that he should be in a wheelchair. He didn't let this change bother him; in fact, he admitted that it enabled him to get around better. His approach to life didn't change. Jane said, "Stephen doesn't make any concessions to his illness, and I don't make any concessions to him."

Hawking recalls when his first black hole breakthrough occurred. In November 1970, he was thinking about black holes while getting ready for bed. As he remembers it: "My disability makes this a rather slow process, so I had plenty of time. Suddenly, I realized that many of the techniques that Penrose and I had developed to prove singularities could be applied to black holes."

Over a six-year period, Hawking co-authored *The Large Scale Structure of Spacetime* with George Ellis. In March 1974, Hawking became a Fellow of the Royal Society at the age of thirty-two. He continued to collect prizes, six major awards in two years: the Eddington Medal from the Royal Astronomical Society, the Pius XI Medal awarded by the Pontifical Academy of Science in the Vatican, the Hopkins Prize, the Dannie Heineman Prize, the Maxwell Prize, and the Hughes Medal of the Royal Society, which cited "his remarkable results in his work on black holes."

In 1978, Hawking was awarded the Albert Einstein Award by the Lewis and Rose Strauss Memorial Fund. During the following year, Hawking co-authored *General Relativity: An Einstein Centenary Survey* with Werner Israel. Hawking was appointed Lucasian Professor at Cambridge University in 1979, 310 years after Isaac Newton was given the same honor. At about this time, an interviewer asked Hawking again about his disability. He responded: "I think I'm happier now than I was before I started. Before the illness set in, I was very bored with life. It really was a rather pointless existence."

Cambridge University Press hoped that Hawking's latest book, *The Very Early Universe,* would sell better than his previous one, *Superspace and Supergravity*, which even scientists had difficulty understanding. The University Press suggested to Hawking that he write a popular book about cosmology. The Press had success previously publishing popular science books by Arthur Eddington and Fred Hoyle.

Hawking was a tough negotiator, and the University Press didn't think that they could afford the generous advance that he demanded. The initial sample of a section of the book that Hawking provided was much too technical. In particular, it contained too many equations. The Press told him that every equation would reduce sales significantly.

Just prior to signing with Cambridge University Press, Hawking was told that Bantam Books was interested in his popular book about cosmology. Bantam offered an advance for the United States and Canada. Bantam's editors also suggested that the technical content of the manuscript should be reduced.

By Christmas, 1984, the first draft of the manuscript was finished. Bantam began to promote the book: "Hawking is on the cutting edge of what we know about the cosmos. This whole business of the unified field theory, the conjunction of relativity with quantum mechanics, is comparable to the search for the Holy Grail."

In 1985, Hawking spent the summer in Geneva, Switzerland, at CERN, the European Center for Nuclear Research, where he continued his research and made corrections to the manuscript of his book. One night in early August, Hawking suffered a blockage in his windpipe and later contracted pneumonia. He was placed on a life-support machine but was not in critical condition. Because he was unable to breathe through his mouth or nose, doctors recommended a tracheostomy. A cut would be made in his windpipe and a breathing device would be implanted. However, Hawking would never be able to speak again.

A California computer technologist, Walt Woltosz, gave Hawking a program called Equalizer that provided a menu of 3,000 words from which to construct sentences. The sentences were sent to a voice-synthesizer that spoke for him with an American accent. Hawking's life was transformed by this technology.

In early spring of 1988, Hawking's popular book about cosmology, *A Brief History of Time: From the Big Bang to Black Holes,* was released. Within a few weeks, this book about equating relativity theory with quantum mechanics was at the top of the best-seller list, where it stayed. Stephen Hawking fan clubs were formed. Sales of the book exceeded everyone's estimates, particularly Bantam's.

More than any previous accomplishment, *A Brief History of Time* made Stephen Hawking a household name. A documentary, "Master of the Universe" won a Royal Television Society award, and ABC presented a profile of Hawking on its 20 / 20 program. Earlier, Commander of the British Empire (CBE) honors had been conferred upon Hawking, and, in 1989, he was made a Companion of Honor by Queen Elizabeth.

Hawking's list of achievements is impressive, particularly when his handicap is considered. However, he has suggested that his accomplishments might not have been as great if he hadn't been diagnosed with ALS at the age of twenty-one. Hawking, a strong-willed individual who was highly motivated, always maintained his sense of humor; his upbeat outlook on life contributed significantly to his success. He observed, "One has to be grown up enough to realize that life is not fair. You have to do the best you can in the situation you are in."

Hawking gave us something to think about in the conclusion of his book, *A Brief History of Time*:

> However, if we do discover a complete theory, it should be in time understandable in broad principle by everyone, not just a few scientists. Then we shall all, philosophers, scientists, and just ordinary people, be able to take part in the discussion of the question of why it is that we and the universe exist. If we find an answer to that, it would be the ultimate triumph of human reason—for then we would know the mind of God.

* * *

Paul Wittgenstein and Stephen Hawking were highly motivated individuals who displayed considerable optimism in overcoming their physical disabilities: Wittgenstein's loss of his right arm and Hawking's nerve degeneration caused by "Lou Gehrig's disease."

Wittgenstein remained optimistic and searched out the few existing concertos for the left hand and commissioned further works to be composed. It is astounding that a person could attend one of his concerts and not be aware that they were listening to a one-armed pianist.

Hawking continued to be productive as his ailment forced him to be less physically active. He observed: "When one's expectations are reduced to zero, one really appreciates everything that one does have. If a person is physically disabled, he or she cannot afford to be psychologically disabled."

CHAPTER 4

PERSUASION / NEGOTIATION—ROLE MODELS

DeWitt Clinton (1769-1828) Father of the Erie Canal

William Seward (1801-1872) Lincoln's Secretary of State

"People smart negotiators use their skills at tuning in and explaining things clearly to encourage acceptance and understanding. Empathy, tact, and humor can go a long way to foster partnership. And when we approach conflict resolution as partners, rather than adversaries, we can avoid wasting time bogging down in extraneous battles, saving our energy for the real issues at hand. The idea is to fix the problem, not the blame."

Mel Silberman, *People Smart*

DEWITT CLINTON—Father of the Erie Canal

"Why sir, here is a canal of a few miles projected by General Washington, which if completed, would render this [Washington, D.C.] a fine commercial city, which has languished for many years, because the small sum of two hundred thousand dollars necessary to complete it cannot be obtained from the General Government, the State Government, or from individuals, and you talk of making a canal 350 miles through the wilderness! It is little short of madness to think of it at this day."

Thomas Jefferson

(The President's reply in January 1809 to Joshua Forman of New York who had requested federal funds to build the Erie Canal. Jefferson thought that it was "a very fine project that might be executed a century hence.")

DeWitt Clinton, the second son of James Clinton and Mary DeWitt Clinton, was born in Little Britain, New York, on March 2, 1769. DeWitt's father, James Clinton, was a major general in the Continental Army and was second-in-command to Major General John Sullivan, who subdued the Iroquois Confederation in his campaign through the Finger Lakes Region in 1779.

In 1786, Clinton graduated first in his class from Columbia College. He studied law, was admitted to the bar, and was authorized to practice before the State Supreme Court. Upon completion of three years of legal training, he became private secretary to his uncle, George Clinton, who was the first Governor of New York. In 1797, Clinton was elected to the State Assembly and the following year to a four-year term in the State Senate.

In February 1802, Clinton was appointed to finish John Armstrong's term in the U. S. Senate. He resigned in October 1803 to become Mayor of the City of New York. With the exception of two years, he was the Mayor of New York from 1803 until 1815. As mayor, he was the organizer of the Public School Society, the patron of the New York Orphan Asylum, and the chief sponsor of the New York City Hospital. While serving as mayor, he also was a State Senator from 1806 until 1811 and Lieutenant-Governor from 1811 until 1813.

In 1815, when Clinton completed his last term as mayor, he devoted himself to promoting the project of building a State canal from the Great Lakes to the Hudson River. A short canal between the Mohawk River and Wood Creek had already been constructed, and the concept of additional canals had been discussed by Gouverneur Morris since 1803. Morris had reviewed his ideas with Simeon DeWitt, who was surveyor general of the State of New York. Both men thought that it was feasible to build a canal across the State.

In 1807, Jesse Hawley of Canandaigua wrote and published a series of essays promoting the construction of a canal from Lake Erie to Utica on the Mohawk River. In 1808, State Legislator Joshua Forman proposed that the Lake Erie canal route should be surveyed. The surveyor general commissioned James Geddes of Syracuse to do the survey. Geddes thought that it would be practical to build a canal across the State as far west as Lake Erie.

Clinton read all of the material about canals that he could find, including Hawley's essays and the history of European waterways. On March 13, 1810, both houses of the State Legislature voted for the formation of the Canal Commission and for an investigation of the practicality of a New York State canal. Clinton was one of seven members of the Canal Commission.

Clinton became a strong supporter of the Erie Canal. He observed: "As an organ of communication between the Hudson, the Mississippi, the St. Lawrence, the Great Lakes of the North and West and their tributary rivers, it will create the greatest inland trade ever witnessed. The City [of New York] will become the granary of the world, the emporium of commerce, the seat of manufacture, the focus of great moneyed operations, and the concentrating point of vast, disposable, and accumulating capital."

In 1811, members of the Canal Commission traveled along the prospective canal routes on horseback. Conditions were primitive, but they wanted to investigate the alternative routes personally. In 1812, Clinton made a strong but unsuccessful run for the Presidency against James Madison on an independent ticket.

On June 3, 1817, the Canal Commission received bids for work on the canal and chose the contractors. That year, Clinton was nominated Governor of New York to succeed Daniel Tompkins who had been elected Vice-President of the United States. On July 4, 1817,

Clinton had the honor of digging the first spadeful of earth at Rome to initiate the construction of the middle section of the canal. Clinton retained the office of Governor until 1822, when he lost the election to Robert Yates; he regained the office in 1824.

On April 12, 1824, as the result of maneuvering by his political opponents, Clinton was removed from his position on the Canal Commission. The maneuver backfired; the populace rebelled at the removal of the canal's strongest proponent from the commission. After all, the project was called "Clinton's Ditch." Ultimately, his strong ability to persuade and negotiate won out.

In 1825, the Erie Canal was completed—about two years after its original scheduled completion date and approximately $2 million over the original cost estimate. Those who had told Clinton that it would be an economic failure were wrong; it was a resounding economic success. On October 26, 1825, Governor DeWitt Clinton presided at the opening of the Erie Canal in ceremonies from Buffalo to New York. Clinton traveled the length of the canal on the leading canalboat, the *Seneca Chief*. The firing of cannons and the cheering of the crowds could be heard all along the route. Two barrels of water were transported from Lake Erie to New York to be poured into the Atlantic Ocean in a "wedding of the waters" ceremony.

Clinton's crowning achievement was sponsoring the construction of the Erie Canal. He was a naturalist and a man of many achievements, including serving as president of the American Academy of the Fine Arts and the New York Historical Society and co-founding the Literary and Philosophical Society. He was also active in the Humane Society, the Lyceum of National History, and the Society for the Promotion of Useful Arts.

Clinton died on February 11, 1828, of a heart attack. He did not attain the highest political office to which he aspired; however, he achieved many of his goals and lived a life of accomplishment.

WILLIAM H. SEWARD—Lincoln's Secretary of State

"Seward was a remarkable, an outstanding figure in his era. Even his foes acknowledged his generosity. It was well said of him that he destroyed his enemies by making them his friends. He appreciated the maxim that half a loaf is better than none, remarking toward the end of his career 'it is always better to accept what can be secured and call in the aid of time to perfect what we have established.' He wanted the United States to compete with Europe for the world's trade and commerce, and something more. Teaching by example, it should lead all the rest in building a happier future for mankind. A practical statesman, he was also a dreamer. This, more than his accomplishments, make him one of the significant figures in American history."

Glyndon G. Van Deusen, William H. Seward

William Henry Seward, Abraham Lincoln's Secretary of State, was born in the hamlet of Florida, Orange County, New York, on May 16, 1801. He was one of five children of Samuel Sweezy Seward and Mary Jennings Seward. Samuel Seward was a doctor, land speculator, and merchant, as well as a county judge and postmaster.

In July 1820, Seward graduated from Union College, where he was a member of the Adelphic Debating Society and Phi Beta Kappa. After graduation, he studied law in Goshen and in New York City. In October 1822, he was admitted to the Bar and, several months later, joined the law practice of Judge Elijah Miller in Auburn.

Judge Miller's daughter, Frances Adeline Miller, had been a classmate of Seward's sister, Cornelia, at Mrs. Willard's Female Seminary in Troy. Seward had met Frances when she visited Cornelia at their home in Orange County. Seward and Frances courted and became engaged during the summer of 1823. On October 20, 1824, they were married at St. Paul's Episcopal Church in Auburn.

On a trip to Niagara Falls, a wheel came off the young couple's wagon in Rochester. A young newspaper editor, Thurlow Weed, came to their assistance, and a lifelong friendship was formed between one who sought office and one who sought power. Seward joined the National Republican party, and, in September 1828, he was elected chairman of the party's young men. From 1828 to 1830, Seward was active in the Anti-Masonic party. In 1830, he won the election as that party's candidate for State Senator. In 1832, he was re-elected to the State Senate.

In 1838, Seward was elected Governor of New York, with considerable help from his campaign manager, Thurlow Weed. Weed was also instrumental in Seward's winning a second term as Governor. Weed pointed toward a national office for Seward. In 1848, their goal was reached when Seward was elected to the U. S. Senate. He was re-elected to the Senate in 1854 and positioned himself for his party's nomination for the Presidency in 1856.

In June 1856, James Buchanan was nominated for President at the Democratic National Convention. Buchanan had just returned home from his post as Minister to the Court of St. James and had the advantage over the other candidates of not being involved in the slave state / free state issues of the previous several years. In June 1856, the Republican Party was only several months old when it held its national convention. When Seward was called "the foremost statesman of America" at the convention, the delegates cheered more loudly than for any other candidate, including for successful nominee John C. Fremont.

Thurlow Weed and Seward's other advisors advised him not to run in 1856. They thought that Buchanan would beat the nominee of a newly established party; they advised Seward to aim for 1860. In hindsight, when Abraham Lincoln beat Seward for the Republican nomination for President in 1860, they realized that their friend's best opportunity had been in 1856.

In a campaign speech for his party's candidates in 1858, Seward referred to the country's two incompatible political systems, one based on slave labor and the other representing free labor. He predicted an "irrepressible conflict" as the country grew and the two systems were in frequent contact. He stated that the country must become either entirely a slaveholding nation or one of free labor. In his opinion, the Democratic Party should be turned out of office because it was a tool of the slaveholders.

In 1860, successful Republican candidate Lincoln's first days in office were trouble-filled because most of his cabinet members thought they would make a better President than he would. His Secretary of State, William H. Seward, shared this opinion.

However, Seward later said of Lincoln, "He is the best of us." Seward was a valuable asset to Lincoln during his transition into the Presidency, particularly in matters of protocol. Seward was loyal to his chief; he survived many delegations to President Lincoln requesting that he dump his Secretary of State.

On the black April day that President Lincoln was shot by John Wilkes Booth, the plot included plans to assassinate Vice-President Andrew Johnson and Secretary of State William Seward. Johnson escaped his fate, but Lewis Payne gained access to Seward's house on the pretext of delivering medicine. Payne insisted on instructing Seward about the medicine and climbed the stairs to Seward's bedroom.

Seward's son, Fred, blocked Payne's entrance to his father's bedroom. He was struck on the head with Payne's pistol, after it misfired. Payne entered Seward's bedroom and stabbed him repeatedly; he wounded him in the face and neck, broke his jaw, and slashed his right cheek. Seward's daughter, Fanny, screamed, alerting his son, Augustus, who wrestled Payne out of the bedroom and down the stairs. Payne fled but was captured later.

Seward and Fred were in serious condition for weeks after the attack. In mid-May, Seward returned to the State Department for brief visits, but could not return to his office full-time until July. President Johnson asked Seward to stay on as Secretary of State; he served until the end of President Johnson's term.

After the Civil War, Seward considered acquisitions for the United States. In the 1840s and 1850s, Russia wanted to retain Russian America, as Alaska was called. Eventually, Russia's plans for expansion became focused on the lower Amur River Valley, which they had just purchased from China. Russia thought that further expansion into Alaska from the United States and Canada was inevitable; furthermore, Alaska was indefensible in time of war. Also, the Russian treasury was in need of an infusion of gold.

During the winter of 1864-65, Hiram Sibley, president of the Western Union Telegraph Company, visited St. Petersburg and was told that Russia was interested in selling Alaska. Sibley conveyed this message to the U.S. Minister to Russia, Henry Clay, who passed it on to Seward. Seward immediately began negotiations with the Russian Minister to the United States, Edward Stoeckl.

Seward was so anxious to prepare the treaty for the Senate that he kept the State Department open all evening on March 29, 1867. By early the next morning, he and Stoeckl had the treaty drawn up, signed, and ready for submission to the Senate. The U. S. purchased Alaska for $7 million, and Seward was criticized for the purchase. Minister Clay appraised the value of Alaska at $50 million.

In 1868, when Ulysses S. Grant was elected President, Seward retired from public office. He made several world tours during the first few years of his retirement. On October 10, 1872, he died at his home at Auburn, while appealing to his family to love one another. He may not have attained his goal of the highest office in the land, but he certainly had a life filled with achievement.

* * *

DeWitt Clinton and William Seward were assertive individuals who were successful politicians. They had considerable ability to persuade and to negotiate: Clinton in convincing the people of New York State to finance the construction of the Erie Canal and Seward in convincing Congress of the value of purchasing Alaska from Russia.

Subsequently, the Erie Canal was recognized as a significant economic success. In fact, construction of the canal put the word "Empire" in Empire State. Seward received much criticism for sponsoring the purchase of "Seward's Folly." As with Clinton's expenditures on the canal, Seward's actions were justified over time.

CHAPTER 5

LEADERSHIP—ROLE MODELS

Horatio Nelson (1758-1805) Victor at the Nile, Copenhagen, and Trafalgar

Duke of Wellington (1769-1852) Defeated Napoleon at Waterloo

"The superior leaders managed to balance a people-oriented personal style with a decisive command role. They did not hesitate to take charge, to be purposeful, assertive, and businesslike. But the greatest difference between average and superior leaders was their emotional style. The most effective leaders were more positive and outgoing, more emotionally expressive and dramatic, warmer and more sociable (including smiling more), friendlier and more democratic, more cooperative, more likeable and 'fun to be with,' more appreciative and trustful, and even gentler than those who were merely average."

Daniel Goleman, *Working with Emotional Intelligence*

HORATIO NELSON—Victor at the Nile, Copenhagen, and Trafalgar

"Wherever the British sailor goes, he carries on the collar of his uniform a memorial of the three great triumphs of his country's greatest admiral, Nelson. But it would not matter if those stripes for the Nile, Copenhagen, and Trafalgar were there or not; the British sailor and all that he stands for is Nelson's monument. The man who smashed Napoleon by sea, who established Britain finally as the undisputed mistress of the seas, whose courage and whose genius were lavishly poured out for the benefit of his country, was indeed worthy of the national sentiment that has made him the greatest of England's heroes.

John Allen, ed., *One Hundred Great Lives*

One of Admiral Lord Horatio Nelson's mentors, Captain William Cornwallis, advised him, "When in doubt, to fight is to err on the right side." Later, Nelson advised his captains, "No captain can do very wrong if he places his ship alongside that of an enemy." Nelson always advocated attack, even when he was outgunned or was at a strategic disadvantage such as at Copenhagen, where he was opposed by Danish forces that could replace their casualties. He was determined to win even if it was no more than refusing to admit defeat.

In 1793, war broke out between England and France. Nelson participated in a raid on the French garrison at Calvi in Corsica. A shot struck the ground near him and forced sand and small particles of gravel into his right eye. He described it as a "little hurt"; however, he never regained sight in the eye.

In 1797, Nelson participated in his first full-scale naval battle at Cape St. Vincent off the coast of Portugal. Nelson engaged seven Spanish ships of the line with his ship, the *HMS Captain*, and distinguished himself during the battle. He was promoted to rear admiral and was given the Order of the Bath.

Nelson's next action was the interception of Spanish treasure ships attempting to enter Santa Cruz, the harbor of Tenerife. Nelson's men attacked the harbor at Santa Cruz and were met with heavy fire from the fort and nearby houses. After one English captain was killed and another was wounded, Nelson came ashore to take personal command. As he was getting out of his boat, he was hit with grapeshot in the right elbow. The bone was shattered, and the arm had to be amputated.

The Battle of the Nile

In March 1798, during Britain's long and painful war with France, Nelson left England in his flagship, *Vanguard,* bound for the Mediterranean. With him sailed Captain Troubridge in *Culloden,* Captain Foley in *Goliath,* Captain Hood in *Zealous,* and Captain Miller in *Theseus* in a squadron that would later go into battle with fourteen ships. Lord St. Vincent, the commander-in-chief, was pleased to welcome the aggressive Nelson, whose arrival gave his commander "new life."

Napoleon wanted to attack England, but he realized that the French Navy was no match for the Royal Navy. Instead, he carried the war to the Mediterranean by attacking and sacking Malta, which was defended by the Knights of St. John, a shadow of their former strength when they had fought in Palestine during the Crusades. Napoleon, who was General of France's Army and Admiral (assisted by Admiral De Brueys) of France's Navy, loaded Malta's treasures on his flagship, *L'Orient,* and sailed for Egypt.

Nelson arrived in Egypt, but because he was short of frigates, the eyes of the fleet, he did not know the location of the French fleet. Napoleon off-loaded his army from his ships at Marabout. Nelson had used the time looking for Napoleon to train his already highly trained fleet. British seamen may not have been well paid, well fed, or well treated, but they were well trained and when they were asked to fight, they fought well. England was justifiably proud of their "hearts of oak."

The French fleet of seventeen ships, which included the flagship (120 guns), three ships of the line (80 guns each) and nine ships of the line (74 guns each), and four frigates (two with 40 guns and two with 36), outmanned Nelson's ships. Nelson had fourteen ships of the line, all with 74 guns except the smaller *Leander,* and no frigates. The difference in weight of metal was significant; a French seventy-four carried heavier guns than a British seventy-four. However, the level of discipline and training was much higher in the British ships.

Admiral De Brueys had anchored at Aboukir Bay, near the mouth of the Nile, because of excessive silt in the bay at Alexandria. De Brueys felt secure because he had shoals on one side of his ships, breakers on the other side, and his frigates positioned on the flanks. Furthermore, French artillery on Bequier Island provided additional cover for his ships, and sunset was only a few hours away when the British fleet was sighted.

Nelson, who had been restless while searching for the French fleet, was eager for a fight. He said, "Before this time tomorrow, I shall have gained a peerage, or Westminster Abbey." Nelson took a substantial risk by attacking a fleet anchored so close to shore; he assumed that the typically conservative French fleet would not risk anchoring too close to the shoreline.

The battle began at 6:30 p.m., at sundown. Early in the battle, Captain Troubridge's *Culloden* went aground. Each of Nelson's ships mounted four lights in a line at the top of the mizzen mast to distinguish them from French ships. Realizing that he was facing an enemy with superior firepower, Nelson's plan of battle was to bring an overpowering force to bear on part of the French line (the van).

Captain Foley, the most experienced of Nelson's captains, in *Goliath,* took the initiative by leading *Zealous, Theseus, Orion,* and *Audacious* between the first ship in the French line, *Le Guerrier,* and the French battery on Bequier Island to position themselves between the shoreline and the French line of ships. These ships brought concentrated fire to bear on the French line, destroying the French ships in the van within two hours of the start of the battle. Captain Darby's ship, *Bellerophon,* had her masts and cables shot away by *L'Orient* and drifted out of control. *Majestic* had many casualties; her Captain, Westcott, was killed.

Admiral De Brueys in *L'Orient* fought on after receiving three wounds, two in the body and one in the head, before being cut in two by the fourth shot. Commodore Casabianca assumed command until *L'Orient,* with all of Malta's treasures, blew up at ten o'clock. The explosion was heard at Alexandria, fifteen miles away.

During the battle, Nelson was struck in the forehead by a piece of iron shot, causing a flap of skin to hang down over his right eye, his blind eye. The three-inch wound in his forehead, which bared his skull, bled profusely, and he was temporarily blinded. Although he was in great pain, when the doctor left the sailor he was treating to attend the admiral, Nelson said, "No, I will take my turn with my brave fellows."

Nelson drafted a report of the battle for Lord St. Vincent and the Lord Commissioners of the Admiralty:

> Nothing could withstand the squadron your Lordships did me the honor to place under my command. Their high state of discipline is well known to you, and with the judgment of the captains, together with their valor, and that of officers and men of every description, it was absolutely irresistible. Could anything from my pen add to the character of the captains I would write it with pleasure, but that is impossible.

Lord Howe wrote to Nelson that he thought it notable that *every* captain had done his duty. Howe had experienced naval battles in which that statement could not have been made. Nelson felt that he owed a description of the battle to Howe, whom he thought was the "first and greatest sea-officer the world has ever produced." "I had the happiness to command a Band of Brothers. Each knew his duty, and I was sure each would feel for a French ship. By attacking the enemy's van and center, the wind blowing directly along their line, I was enabled to throw what force I pleased on a few ships. We always kept a superior force to the enemy."

Of the seventeen ships in Admiral De Bruey's fleet, all but four were either on fire or flying the British Union Jack the next morning. Nelson had not lost a single ship; it was the most complete victory that the Royal Navy had ever experienced. The French had six times the casualties, 5225, of the British, including men who were missing or captured. The Admiralty, which had been criticized for choosing a young admiral like Nelson for such an important command, was justified in its choice. England was overjoyed with Nelson's victory; he was raised to the peerage with the title Baron Nelson of the Nile.

Battle of Copenhagen

In 1801, Admiral Nelson embarked to the Baltic with a fleet under the command of Admiral Sir Hyde Parker. Denmark, Sweden, and

Russia had joined in an alliance against England called the League of Neutrality because England, during the war with France, had interfered with their shipping. The League of Neutrality was a stance of armed neutrality in which England was denied the right of "visit and search" that they had always demanded. Russia was the leader of the league, and Emperor Paul I of Russia had imposed an embargo on English shipping in his ports. Also, France pressured Denmark and Sweden to use their navies against England.

Nelson wanted to attack the Russian port of Reval. However, he was second-in-command to Sir Hyde Parker, an elderly, conservative admiral close to retirement who didn't want healthy Danish and Swedish fleets between him and England. The English had a choice of attacking these potential enemies before they assumed the initiative or relying on the presence of a large Royal Navy fleet and using threatening language to subdue the League.

The British decided to destroy the Danish fleet at Copenhagen. Earlier attempts to negotiate with the Danes had merely given the Danes more time to prepare for battle. Nelson suggested that they strike at once. Admiral Parker's hesitation was understandable; the Danes had fortified Copenhagen harbor heavily.

The harbor couldn't be approached from the North because of the Trekroner (three crowns) fort with over seventy guns. South of the fort, the Danes had dismasted and moored eighteen men-of-war with a total of 634 guns in a line one and a half miles in length along the inner or King's Channel. Immediately in front of the harbor was the Middle Ground, a shoal that prevented a straight-in approach. The English would have to enter the harbor in a single file but couldn't use their heavy ships, which had too much draft to negotiate the channel.

Only the light ships of the line, along with frigates, could be used in the harbor; Admiral Parker, with the heavy ships of the line, positioned himself to prevent any Swedish or Russian ships from coming to the aid of the Danes. To make navigation by the enemy difficult, the Danes had removed all of the buoys from the channel. Soundings were taken, and the buoys were replaced under the personal supervision of Admiral Nelson during the evening before the battle.

Nelson shifted his flag from his flagship, the *St. George*, to the lighter *Elephant* (74 guns) commanded by Captain Foley, who had led the line at the Battle of the Nile. In Nelson's plan of battle, twelve ships of the line would fight in the harbor while the frigates, under Captain Riou, would be held in reserve.

The battle started badly for the British, when the second ship of the line, *Agamemnon*, went aground on the Middle Ground Shoal. Two other ships of the line, the *Bellona* and the *Russell*, went aground attempting to maneuver around the shoal.

The nine ships that made it into position provided cover for the three ships that went aground. Initially, neither the end of the Danish line nor the Danish fort had any opposition. Captain Riou attempted to take on the end of the Danish line with his frigates and was met with extremely heavy fire. The Danes had the advantage of being able to row men out to the hulks to replace those who were killed or wounded.

The guns of Admiral Parker's ships were out of range and could not help Nelson's ships. Parker could see that Nelson was taking a pounding; the Danes' fire was more accurate than anticipated.

The Danes proved to be tough opponents. Finally, Admiral Parker decided to discontinue the action. He sent his flag captain, Captain Otway, to go aboard Nelson's ship, *Elephant*, to find out what was happening.

Before Captain Otway could report back to Sir Hyde, the Commander-in-chief flew signal number thirty-nine to leave off action. Nelson continued flying signal number sixteen, the signal for close action. Nelson looked at Parker's signal to leave off action, turned to Captain Foley, captain of the *Elephant*, and said, "You know Foley, I only have one eye. I have a right to be blind sometimes." Then he raised his telescope to his right eye, his blind eye, and said, "I really do not see the signal."

After five hours of heated conflict, a truce was granted, and both sides tended their wounded. The casualties were heavy; however, the Danish casualties were many times the English casualties of just under a thousand men. Truce negotiations dragged on, but, finally, the Battle of Copenhagen was declared an important victory for the English. The battle was won because Nelson refused to stop fighting and admit defeat.

The Battle of Trafalgar

In the fall of 1805, Nelson prepared for what would be his last battle. Under his command were twenty-seven ships of the line, four frigates, a schooner, and a cutter. His squadron included Admiral Collingwood (his second in command) in *Royal Sovereign,* Captain Berry in *Agamemnon*, Captain Harvey in *Téméraire*, and Captain Freemantle in *Neptune.* Captain Hardy, Nelson's friend, commanded *Victory,* his flagship.

Admiral Villeneuve, in command of the combined French and Spanish fleet at Trafalgar, instructed the captains under his command of Nelson's intentions: "He will try to double our rear, cut through the line, and bring against the ships thus isolated groups of his own, to surround and capture them. Captains must rely on their courage and love of glory, rather than the signals of the Admiral, who may already be engaged and wrapped in smoke. The captain who is not in action is not at his post." Nelson's written instructions to his captains were similar to what Villeneuve had expected:

> The order of sailing was to be the order of battle. The second in command, Admiral Collingwood, after Nelson's intentions had been made known by signal, would have entire direction of the line. If possible he was to cut through the enemy about the twelfth ship from the rear. The remainder of the combined fleet was to be left to the management of the commander-in-chief, whose endeavor would be to see that, while the rear was pulverized by Collingwood, no interference should be encountered from the van.

Villeneuve commanded thirty-three ships of the line (eighteen French and fifteen Spanish), five French frigates, and two brigs. During the evening of October 19, the brig *Argus* notified Villeneuve on the French flagship, *Bucentaure,* that eighteen British ships had been sighted.

Prior to going into battle, Nelson thought of his family. He wrote a document asking his country to provide for his beloved wife Emma Hamilton "that they will give her an ample provision to maintain her rank in life," and he also left "to the beneficence of my country my adopted daughter, Horatia."

At six o'clock the next morning, Nelson signaled his fleet from his flagship, *Victory,* to form into two columns while sailing toward the combined French and Spanish fleets. Nelson's officers on the *Victory* convinced him that the flagship should not be the first ship to go into action. He seemed to agree to let *Téméraire* go into action ahead of *Victory;* however, *Victory* did not give way, and Nelson hailed *Téméraire* from the quarterdeck, "I'll thank you, Captain Harvey, to keep your proper station, which is astern of *Victory.*"

Nelson signalled his squadron, "England expects that every man will do his duty," followed by the signal for close action. Collingwood in *Royal Sovereign* went into action well ahead of his squadron, cutting the line of the combined fleet just astern of the *Santa Anna,* Admiral Alava's flagship.

Gunfire from the topmasts of the combined fleets' *Redoubtable* rained down on the deck of *Victory* until *Téméraire* came up to support *Victory.* At 1:15 p.m., Hardy saw Nelson, on his knees, fall to the deck. He told Hardy, "They have done for me at last, Hardy." A shot from the fighting tops of *Redoubtable* had shattered Nelson's left shoulder, penetrated his chest, and lodged in his spine.

Nelson was carried below. Hardy visited Nelson to give him status of the battle: "We have got twelve or fourteen of the enemy's ships in our possession but five of their van have tacked, and show an intention of bearing down on *Victory.* I have therefore called two or three of our fresh ships around us, and we are giving them a drubbing."

Hardy returned to his duty station to send Collingwood a message about the severity of Nelson's wound. He visited Nelson about an hour later. Nelson asked Hardy to "take care of my dear Lady Hamilton, Hardy; take care of poor Lady Hamilton. Kiss me, Hardy." After Hardy had kissed his cheek, Nelson said, "Now I am satisfied. Thank God, I have done my duty." Before returning to the deck, Hardy bent down again and kissed his dying friend on the forehead. Nelson died at 4:30 p.m.

Nelson had won another overwhelming victory. Villeneuve was a prisoner, his combined fleet was scattered, and no British ships had been lost. Nelson was mourned by an appreciative nation. Nelson's body was shipped home and on December 23 was transported up the Thames River to Greenwich, where it lay in state in Christopher Wren's Painted Hall in a coffin made from timber from *L'Orient.* The body was taken to Whitehall and the Admiralty and finally to St. Paul's Cathedral for burial.

Collingwood became a peer, and Hardy was made a baronet. *Victory* was repaired and saw further service in the war against Napoleon. *Victory* was restored and then restored again after being struck by a bomb during World War II; the ship is a popular attraction for visitors to England.

DUKE OF WELLINGTON—Defeated Napoleon at Waterloo

"Hard pounding this, gentlemen; let's see who will pound the longest."

Duke of Wellington at Waterloo

In April 1815, just prior to the Battle of Waterloo, George Canning said to Lord Castlereagh, "what a happy consummation of his [Wellington's] story it would be to put the last hand to the destruction of Bonaparte's power in direct conflict with Bonaparte." Wellington did, and it was.

On April 5, 1815, the Duke of Wellington assumed command in Brussels, Belgium, of the joint forces of Great Britain and the Netherlands. His mission, with these joint forces and a Prussian Army, was to perform advance guard duties until they could be joined by armies from Austria and Russia.

The British contingent of his army was comprised of six cavalry regiments and twenty-five infantry battalions, approximately 14,000 men. Half of these men had never been in battle. Most of Wellington's Peninsular Army, which had fought in Portugal and Spain, had been demobilized. Many of those who hadn't been demobilized had fought in the War of 1812 in the United States or were en route from there. The other half of his army was made up of combined Dutch and Belgian forces who were less experienced and less dependable than his British contingent.

Wellington's forces expanded to 60,000 by the end of April and to 90,000 by mid-June. He organized his army into three corps and strengthened his green units by placing British or King's German Legion troops alongside inexperienced men. Wellington and General Blucher, commander of the Prussian Army, defended a front that extended over one hundred miles, from Liege to Tournai. Apprehension of attack by Napoleon diminished as the Allied Army added units. The Prussian Army grew to approximately 113,000 by mid-June, but was spread out from Charleroi to the Ardennes Forest; the smaller British-Netherlands-German Legion Army manned the frontier from the North Sea to Mons.

On the evening of June 15, the Duchess of Richmond gave a ball in Brussels that was attended by most senior officers of the Allied Armies, including the Duke of Wellington and the Prince of

Orange, who commanded the Netherlands contingent. Wellington had insisted on attending the ball in an attempt to prevent civilians from fleeing the Belgian capital in panic.

Several times during the evening, Wellington received messages and wrote and sent orders. Many of his staff left the ball early, reacting to the news that at dawn that morning Napoleon with approximately 124,000 men had crossed the Sambre River and attacked the right wing of Blucher's army near where it joined the left wing of Wellington's army.

The initial communication from Blucher that had been received in mid-afternoon was sketchy and no longer current. Wellington couldn't commit the bulk of his forces until he knew which of three roads to Brussels—through Charleroi, through Mons, or through Tournai—Napoleon was going to use. Before he left the ball, Wellington had heard that the attack on the Prussians was a serious one, and he ordered a concentration of his forces at Quatre-Bras near Nivelles, several miles west of the Charleroi-Brussels road.

By mid-afternoon on Friday, June 16, the left wing of Napoleon's army, commanded by Marshal Ney, almost over-whelmed the forces of the Prince of Orange at Quatre-Bras. During the afternoon, one British division unsupported by cavalry held off three of Ney's divisions with 4,000 cavalrymen.

Wellington personally directed the defense; he issued tactical orders to every battalion and even to selected companies. He was an energetic general in the prime of his life and an active partici-pant in the action.

While trying to rally a light cavalry unit, Wellington was sur-rounded by French lancers. He escaped by jumping his chestnut horse, Copenhagen, a veteran of the Peninsular Campaign, over a ditch filled with infantry, bayonets and all. Eventually, when addi-tional allied troops joined the battle, Wellington took the offensive and drove back Ney's forces. However, Wellington's ally, Blucher, with 80,000 Prussians, was beaten back at Ligny by 63,000 sea-soned French troops. In another close call, Blucher was almost cap-tured by the French cavalry when they overran his position.

Napoleon detached a force of 33,000 under Marshal Grouchy to pursue the Prussians as they withdrew northward toward Wavre. Napoleon's directive to Grouchy was contradictory. In an earlier communication, Grouchy had indicated his intention of pursuing the Prussians to separate them from Wellington's army. However, Napoleon's orders were: "His Majesty desires you will head for Wavre in order to draw near to us." The portion of the message with which Grouchy complied was the order, "head for Wavre." This virtually ensured that these 33,000 men wouldn't be available to Napoleon at Waterloo.

During Saturday morning, Napoleon pressured Wellington, who withdrew in an orderly fashion to the ridge of Mont St. Jean, twelve miles south of Brussels. Wellington maintained communications with his Prussian Allies, who were only twelve miles to the east. Wellington knew well the ridge to which he had retired; he had studied it as a potential site for a battle. The ridge had places to conceal his troops on the reverse slopes and a forest behind them extended for miles, providing a refuge for his green troops if they needed it. Wellington had to maintain a defensive position, since he couldn't do complicated maneuvers with his relatively untrained troops.

Wellington realized that coordination of his combined army and the Prussian Army was crucial. Together they could defeat Napoleon; separately they couldn't. Wellington continued to sprinkle seasoned British and German Legion troops throughout his less seasoned units. He employed his less dependable units and those units with heavy casualties as guards for his flanks and as reserves. Wellington located his principal reserve behind his right flank to the west under the command of his most reliable corps commander, General "Daddy" Hill.

Wellington placed his main force on the reverse slope of the hill and positioned his artillery, which had smaller and fewer cannons than the French, along the ridge. Then he hid his skirmishers in the cornfields on the forward slope of the hill, ensuring that the French would have to move through three lines of fire. Wellington had several units, including General Clinton's 2nd [Infantry] Division, that were extremely maneuverable and operated like light infantry divisions. He maintained good communications and moved units quickly to the weak points.

Napoleon was confident of victory that day, as he had been against the Prussians with their superior numbers on the previous day. He was sure that many of Wellington's less well-trained units would break and run when confronted with his veterans. Napoleon outlined his plan of battle: "I shall hammer them with my artillery, charge them with my cavalry to make them show themselves, and, when I am quite sure where the actual English are, I shall go straight at them with my Old Guard."

On Sunday, June 18, around noon, Napoleon opened the fighting with a feint at Hougoumont to the east. Prince Jerome's French troops were beaten back; a second diversion was made at the same location with a larger body of troops. Then Prince Jerome attempted to take Hougoumont a third time. Wellington held on by dispatching four companies of the Life Guards to enforce the position.

The feint at Hougoumont was the first phase of the Battle of Waterloo. Napoleon massed the main body of his troops at the center, where he planned his principal attack. When the French bombardment began, Napoleon observed troop movements about five or six miles away toward Wavre. At first he thought they were Grouchy's troops sent to pursue the Prussians. Then he realized what Wellington already knew; they were Blucher's troops hurrying to rejoin Wellington. He decided to make a frontal attack on the center. Napoleon would deal with Wellington first, then with Blucher. He sent reserves to delay the Prussians.

The second phase of the battle began at one o'clock when the French began a bombardment with eighty guns, including twenty-four of the dreaded twelve-pounders. The cannonade was intense, but it inflicted minimal casualties due to Wellington's disposition of the men on the reverse slope of the ridge.

At 1:30 p.m., Count D'Erlon ordered the French right to attack. The grenadiers attacked to the beating of drums in a formation of four hundred shouting men abreast. They were met, but not stopped, by Wellington's artillery. The French overran and isolated the Germans defending La Haye Saint, who were driven from their position in an orchard. The fighting at the crest of the ridge was critical. Sir Thomas Picton's division was ordered to advance to meet D'Erlon's attack. Picton's division was led by his Peninsular commanders, Pack and Kempt, and was made up of veterans. Sir Dennis Pack ordered the Gordons, the Blackwatch, and the 44th forward; Sir Thomas Picton led Kempt's line personally, until a bullet pierced the top hat that he wore in battle and struck him in the temple. He was killed instantly.

Wellington ordered Lord Uxbridge to charge with the Household and Union Brigades of heavy cavalry, under Lord Edward Somerset on the right and Sir William Ponsonby on the left. The Union Brigade was composed of the Royal Dragoons, the Scots Greys, and the Inniskillings from Ireland. Wellington personally led the Life Guards in the advance. Wellington's heavy cavalry carried away everything in its path. The awe-inspiring charge routed a sizable body of French infantry in formation. However, Uxbridge was unable to control the charge. The cavalry overran its positions, and then went on the defensive with substantial loss of life. The heavy cavalry wasn't an effective fighting force for the remainder of the battle. Wellington lost 2,500 cavalrymen in this charge, about one quarter of those available to him.

The third phase of the battle began with an act of poor judgement by Marshal Ney. He decided that taking the central section of the ridge was his responsibility, and that he would do it with cavalry alone. Napoleon's cavalry was nearly as numerous as the British infantry. Wellington was astounded to see the French heavy cavalry, one of the world's finest, forming up to advance upon the allied infantry without infantry support.

Wellington ordered his 1st and 3rd divisions opposite the point of attack to form battalion squares in a checkerboard fashion, such that the front edge of each square had a clear field of fire with respect to the next square. He ordered his men to lie down in the cornfields on the plateau until the French cavalry came within range. Between the squares, Wellington placed his last two reserve batteries of Horse Artillery. Their nine-pounders were filled with double loads of anti-personnel grapeshot. Behind the squares, he placed his cavalry, including the remnants of the two brigades of heavy cavalry that Lord Uxbridge had been unable to control.

The French cavalry came at the Allied squares in formation at a controlled pace. The British artillery caused havoc along the line of advancing cavalry; horses were down all over the central portion of the plateau. The allied infantry held their fire and then fired upon order in unison. The results were devastating. Ney varied the attack, but the British and Hanover infantry remained cool and unyielding. The French cavalry approached the squares from the sides and, at one point, from the rear. Napoleon's cavalry charged the battalion squares five times without success. Wellington may not have been able to maneuver with his relatively inexperienced army, but he could rely on them to hold a position with tenacity under heavy fire.

Although Napoleon and Wellington were both in their mid-forties, Napoleon, unlike Wellington, hadn't played an active role in the battle until this point. Early in the day, Napoleon studied the battlefield and issued orders to his Marshals. Then, in effect, he delegated control of the offensive to Marshal Ney. Napoleon was fatigued from the strenuous activity of the last three days and was suffering from hemorrhoids. He spent several hours of the afternoon lying down at his headquarters at Rossomme in a semi-comatose state. Napoleon roused himself and took over direction of the battle from Ney. He was ready to direct another victory as he had done so many times before. He moved forward to La Belle-Alliance and ordered Ney to take the farm at La Haye Sainte.

The farm at La Haye Sainte was defended by fewer than four hundred men of the King's German Legion commanded by a British officer, Major George Baring. They had started the day with sixty rounds of ammunition per man, but were down to four or five rounds each. Their appeals for more ammunition had gone unheeded. Two light companies were the only reinforcement they received. When their ammunition ran out, they defended the farm with bayonets. The only survivors of La Haye Saint were Major Baring and forty-two men who fought their way through the French lines with their bayonets.

Just after six o'clock, Ney renewed the attack on the allied center with two columns of infantry and cavalry which were driven back by the British artillery. Wellington reformed Clinton's veteran division from the reserve and Chasse's Hollanders from the west behind the center of the line. Also, he reduced the squares to four deep to allow increased firepower against infantry but to retain their effectiveness against the reduced cavalry threat.

The young Prince of Orange was in charge of the center of the line. On two occasions, he had deployed Ompteda's battalions of King's German Legion against cavalry with disastrous results. A breakthrough of the center of the allied line was averted only by a charge of the 3rd Hussars of the German Legion and the accurate firepower of the 1st battalion of the 95th Rifles. Ney noted that the center was vulnerable. He asked Napoleon for more men to exploit the opportunity. Napoleon asked Ney if he expected him to create them. Napoleon had twelve battalions of the Imperial Guard still in reserve, but he wasn't ready to commit everything at this point.

Wellington was aware of the dilemma that confronted him. He assigned every reserve that he could muster to shore up his crumbling center, including five inexperienced Brunswick battalions and Vivian's light cavalry. The artillery fire from both sides was intense. The young Brunswickers began to break, but were rallied by Wellington's personal effort.

Wellington rode up to Sir Alexander Frazer, commander of the Horse Artillery, and said, "Twice have I saved this day by perseverance." Wellington was known to be modest about his abilities. However, Frazer agreed with the observation and noted that Wellington was "cool and indifferent at the beginning of battles but when the moment of difficulty comes, intelligence flashes from the eyes of this wonderful man and he rises superior to all that can be imagined." Lord Uxbridge, Wellington's deputy commander, who hadn't served with him previously, told Lady Shelley, "I thought I had heard enough of this man but he has far surpassed my expectations. He is not a man but a god."

Napoleon, who was about three-quarters of a mile away from the line, and Wellington could both see Blucher's Prussian 1st Corps commanded by General Zieten about two miles away hurrying to Wellington's aid. Earlier, Zieten had been informed by a Prussian staff officer that Wellington was withdrawing when he saw the allied army retiring to the ridge. The staff officer ordered the Prussian 1st Corps to retrace their steps and to move toward Blucher. General Muffling told Zieten that the battle would be lost if the 1st Corps didn't go to Wellington's aid. Zieten ordered his Prussians back toward Wellington.

Napoleon, having missed his chance to break the allied center, realized that the moment of crisis had come. He ordered aides to carry the word that the men in the distance were Grouchy's coming to his aid, not Blucher's coming to support Wellington. Shortly after seven o'clock, Napoleon committed his Imperial Guard, and the final phase of the battle began.

Napoleon issued a general order for all units to advance and delegated Ney to lead the attack. The Imperial Guards moved toward the ridge in two columns, one advancing toward the center of the allied right and one climbing between Hougoumont and the center. Wellington placed himself at the point at which the main blow was aimed—to the right of the Life Guards. As he had done previously, he ordered his men to lie down in the corn fields until the Imperial Guard was within rifle range. Wellington's artillery was particularly effective against the front ranks of the Imperial guards and caused many casualties, including many of the Old Guard's seasoned officers. Ney walked up the hill after his fifth mount was shot out from under him.

As he had done earlier with Vivian's cavalry, Wellington placed Vandeleur's cavalry behind some of his less seasoned units, that is, between them and the woods behind them. This created a steadying influence on the younger units. When Wellington gave the order to stand and fire, advance units of the Imperial Guards were only twenty yards away. The results of fifteen hundred men firing at close range was devastating. The Imperial Guards reeled, but they didn't break. They reformed and returned heavy fire assisted effectively by the French artillery.

At this point, Colonel John Colbourne, commanding the first battalion of the 52nd, made a maneuver on his own initiative that played a decisive role in the last phase of the battle. He moved his battalion forward about 300 yards in front of the line and, as it encountered the leading units of the advancing French, ordered a pivoting movement to the left, thus facing the flank of the Imperial Guard. Colbourne risked leaving a gap in the line, and he also risked being cut down by the French Cavalry. However, his daring move paid off; the initial fire from the Imperial Guard took down one hundred and forty men of his battalion, but the 52nd's return fire was so effective that the Imperial Guard broke and fled.

Napoleon's Old Guard, which had never been defeated, turned and ran. When the battered remnants of Napoleon's army saw the Imperial Guard in flight, they turned around and joined them. Dusk was near, and Wellington waved his men on to pursue the retreating Frenchmen. He realized that this was the crucial moment of victory. He ordered Vivian's and Vandeleur's cavalry in pursuit, joined by Zieten's Prussian cavalry from the east. The rout was complete; many of Napoleon's men stacked their arms and ran to the rear.

Wellington met his ally, Blucher, at nine o'clock, in the advancing darkness, between LaBelle Alliance and Rossomme, the two sites at which Napoleon had spent most of his day. Blucher greeted his comrade in arms with "Mein lieber comrade." Wellington responded with "Quelle affaire" since he didn't speak German, and he knew that Blucher didn't speak English. His greeting was in the language of the army he had just beaten. Wellington's personal view of his battles was:

> I look upon Salamanca, Vitoria, and Waterloo as my three best battles—those which had great and permanent consequences. Salamanca relieved the whole south of Spain, changed all of the prospects of the war—it was felt even in Prussia; Vitoria freed the Peninsula altogether, broke off the armistice at Dresden and thus led to Leipzig and the deliverance of Europe; and Waterloo did more than any other battle I know toward the true object of all battles—the peace of the world.

* * *

Lord Horatio Nelson and the Duke of Wellington were persevering individuals: Nelson in the Battles of the Nile, Copenhagen, and Trafalgar and Wellington in his campaign in the Iberian Peninsula and certainly at Waterloo. Aggressiveness was another trait possessed by these leaders. Both leaders were superior strategists: Nelson in forming his ships to engage the enemy in small groups and Wellington in the placement and utilization of his forces at Waterloo.

CHAPTER 6

EMOTIONAL CONTROL—ROLE MODELS

Brigham Young (1801-1877) Led the Mormons to the Salt Lake Valley

Nelson Mandela (1918-   ) First Native-African President of the Union of South Africa

"Managing your emotions means understanding them and then using that understanding to deal with situations productively. Because emotions are produced by an interaction of your thoughts, physiological changes, and behavioral actions in response to an external event, you can manage your emotions by taking charge of each component. Then, because a distressful emotion is generally caused by a problem situation . . . we look next at how you can bring your emotional thermostat to a level that allows you to think productively. You can then use problem solving to come up with the best course of action to take to resolve the situation."

Hendrie Weisinger, *Emotional Intelligence at Work*

BRIGHAM YOUNG —Led the Mormons to the Salt Lake Valley

"Brigham Young is remembered as a dynamic religious leader and hardy pioneer who led the Mormons to the great basin in 1847. As a colonizer, he displayed remarkable leadership and business ability and was largely responsible for the settling of the vast Intermountain West stretching from Canada southward into the heart of Mexico. In addition to being instrumental in establishing numerous communities, he pioneered in the construction of railroads, highways, telegraph lines, irrigation systems, churches, and tabernacles. And he established forts, factories, mines, banks, and stores."

Richard F. Palmer and Karl D. Butler, *Brigham Young*

Historian Oscar Handlin described the role of Brigham Young in opening up the West:

> When a furious mob murdered [Mormon founder Joseph] Smith, Young assumed the leadership of the Mormon survivors and redirected their vision toward new goals. Far beyond the Mississippi, in heretofore unsettled territory, lay the Great Basin to which he led the remnants of the Church and its followers. There Young supervised the building of a new society that soon attracted thousands of newcomers from other parts of the Union and from Europe as well.
>
> The account of this life is thus an American success story, a rise from poor beginnings to power and wealth. But it is also a story that illuminates important features of the social history of the United States—religious enthusiasm, the pioneering spirit, and the encounter with the American West.

Brigham Young, the sixth child and third son of John and Abigail Howe Young, was born on June 1, 1801, in Whitingham, Vermont. John Young was a farmer who moved frequently because of increasingly worn-out soil.

In 1802, John Young moved his family to Smyrna, New York. John cleared land for farming and built a log dwelling. At an early age, Brigham was introduced to hard work, including logging and driving a team of horses. The family was poor and hired Brigham out to neighbors to earn additional income.

The Youngs were Methodists who originally had been New England Congregationalists. In Brigham's opinion, his parents were "the most strict religionists that lived upon the earth." Brigham held back from joining the Methodist church or any other church. He said a prayer to himself: "Lord, preserve me until I am old enough to have sound judgment, and a discreet mind ripened on a good, solid foundation of common sense."

Abigail Young died on June 11, 1815, just after Brigham's fourteenth birthday. He had been close to his mother; in his words, "Of my mother—she that bore me—I can say no better woman lived in the world." Brigham developed into an independent individual with a deliberate manner.

In 1817, John Young married Hannah Dennis Brown, a widow with several children of her own. He broke up his household and moved in with his new wife. Sixteen-year-old Brigham's father told him: "You now have your time; go and provide for yourself."

Young moved to Auburn, where he became an apprentice to learn the trades of carpentry, glazing, and painting. In 1823, Young moved to Port Byron, a fast-growing town on the new Erie Canal. He worked in a furniture repair shop, a wool carding mill, a pail factory, and a boatyard. One of Young's employers observed that he "would do more work in a given time and secure more and better work from his help without trouble than any man they have ever employed."

In 1828, Young moved to Oswego, where he worked on the construction of a large tannery. When the tannery was finished the following year, he moved to Mendon, where his father and several of his sisters had settled. While living in Port Byron, Young heard "rumors of a new revelation, to the effect of a new Bible written upon golden plates at Palmyra. I was somewhat acquainted with the coming forth of the Book of Mormon through the newspapers [and] many stories and reports circulated as the Book of Mormon was printed and scattered abroad."

In June 1830, Young saw a copy of the Book of Mormon when Samuel Smith, a brother of Joseph Smith who had found the golden plates on Hill Cumorah, visited Mendon to preach about Mormonism and to sell copies of the "golden Bible."

In January 1830, Young, his brother, Phineas, and his good friend and neighbor, Heber Kimball, traveled to Columbia, Pennsylvania, the location of the nearest Mormon church, to observe Mormons interpreting their religion, prophesying, and speaking in tongues.

On April 14, Brigham Young was baptized by Elder Eleazer Miller in the stream behind his home. He said that before his clothes "were dry on my back [Elder Miller] laid his hands on me and ordained me an Elder, at which I marveled. According to the words of the Savior, I felt a humble, childlike spirit, witnessing unto me that my sins were forgiven." Ordination as an Elder gave Young the authority to preach the gospel. The rest of the family followed him in joining the new religion.

Four things that Young liked about Mormonism were its similarities to Puritanism, with its emphasis on common sense; its espousal of "Christian Primitivism," the restoration of Christianity as it existed at the time of Jesus Christ; its authoritarianism, which required unquestioning loyalty to the Mormon prophet Joseph Smith; and its lay priesthood, which provided a path to status and influence.

In the fall of 1832, Young and his friend, Heber Kimball traveled to the main Mormon settlement in Kirtland, Ohio, just east of Cleveland, to meet Joseph Smith—founder of the Church of Jesus Christ of Latter-Day Saints. Upon meeting the charismatic Mormon prophet, Young spoke in tongues and asked the Latter-Day Saints leader's opinion of his gift of tongues. Smith "told them that it was of the pure Adamic language. It is of God, and the time will come when brother Brigham Young will preside over this church."

Young returned to Mendon to preach Mormonism and traveled around upstate New York and Canada baptizing converts. In September 1833, he moved to Kirtland to be near Joseph Smith and the center of Mormon activity. He courted Mary Ann Angell, a former Baptist from Seneca, New York. In February 1834, Young and Mary Ann were married by Sidney Rigdon, an influential Mormon leader. Early the following year, Smith appointed Young one of the Council of Twelve Apostles, modeled on the Apostles of the New Testament, who were responsible for overseeing Mormon churches and missionary activity.

From 1835 through 1837, Young traveled around upstate New York, New England, and Canada spreading the word of Mormonism. On a return visit to Kirtland during this time, he supervised the completion of the Kirtland Temple. Smith encountered difficulties in Kirtland when he attempted to establish his own bank. Because of his indebtedness and his plan to print his own money, Smith was denied a State banking charter. He established the bank anyway; unfortunately, it was adversely affected by the Panic of 1837.

In 1838, Young was drawn into the conflict between Mormons and non-Mormons in Missouri. Non-Mormons were concerned about the Mormons' economic and political power in the region. A series of armed clashes began in Gallatin, Missouri, when non-Mormons attempted to prevent Mormons from voting. Three Mormons were killed at Crooked River, Caldwell County, and seventeen Mormons were killed and fifteen wounded seriously at Haun's Mill, Caldwell County, by an unruly mob of over 200 men.

The Governor of Missouri, Lilburn Boggs, called out the Missouri militia and issued the order that Mormons "must be exterminated or driven from Missouri, if necessary, for the public good." Joseph Smith turned himself in to the authorities and his brother, Hyrum, and Sidney Rigdon were arrested. Young was the only senior member of the Council of the Twelve Apostles who was not in captivity. He appealed to the Missouri Legislature for compensation for Mormon property that had been seized. The Mormons received a token payment and, due to threats to their lives, left Missouri for Illinois.

In 1839, Young made his last visit to upstate New York while en route to a successful mission that more than doubled church membership in England. He promoted the increase in the number of English Elders and the immigration of English Mormons to the United States. During the next six years, over 4,000 Mormons immigrated to the United States from Great Britain. He also established a Mormon periodical, the *Millennial Star,* in England. Young clearly established a reputation as an efficient administrator and organizer.

Smith escaped from his six-month captivity and established the center of Mormon faith in Nauvoo, Illinois. In July 1841, when Young returned to Nauvoo, he found that it had become a rapidly growing city of 3,000; it would expand to 10,000 by the end of 1841. The Nauvoo Charter gave Mormons comprehensive powers of self-government, although they could not pass any laws contrary to the Illinois and U.S. Constitutions. The mayor and city council formed their own municipal court, and the city controlled its own militia, the Nauvoo Legion.

Young was elected to the Nauvoo city council and was appointed editor of the Nauvoo newspaper, *The Times and Seasons.* His commitment to Mormonism was severely tested in 1841, when Joseph Smith endorsed the practice of polygamy for the Latter-Day Saints. Initially, Young was appalled by the practice. He said that it "was the first time in my life that I had desired the grave." When he expressed his views to Smith, he was told, "Brother Brigham, the Lord will reveal it to you." Young was faced with the dilemma of either practicing polygamy or defying the prophet Joseph Smith. Eventually, he accepted plural marriage.

The practice of polygamy was the greatest source of difficulty for the Mormons, both within and outside of the church. Nauvoo was envied as the most prosperous city in Illinois, but its self-government was not easily accepted by non-Mormons. Smith realized that he must look to the Far West as "a place of refuge" where "the devil cannot dig us out." In February 1844, Smith asked the Council of Twelve to send a delegation westward toward California and Oregon to build a temple and to establish a government of their own.

The delegation to the West was delayed by Smith's decision to run for the Presidency of the U.S. in 1844 as an independent candidate. Young and other Mormon leaders did much of the campaigning for the candidate. Smith had problems of his own back in Nauvoo, however. A group of dissidents led by William Law split off from the Latter-Day Saints due to disagreements with Smith's policies, particularly polygamy. Law and his associates established a competing newspaper, the Nauvoo *Expositor*. Smith asked the city council to destroy the press and all copies of the newspaper, a blatant violation of freedom of the press.

Anti-Mormon feeling intensified around Nauvoo, and Smith, his brother, Hyrum, and two other Mormon leaders gave themselves up to county authorities in Carthage. On June 27, 1844, a large, organized mob entered the jail at Carthage, killed Smith and his brother, and wounded another of the Mormon leaders. Young, who was campaigning for Smith in Massachusetts at the time, returned to Nauvoo by a roundabout route to avoid assassination.

Young's only serious rival for the Mormon presidency was Sidney Rigdon. Young's forceful speech, his alignment with the Council of Twelve, and his confidence that the Church would make the right decision made him the clear choice. Anti-Mormon sentiment continued to run high, and Illinois Governor Thomas Ford repealed the Nauvoo charter, which disfranchised both the city police and the Nauvoo Legion. Earlier, he had ordered the Nauvoo Legion to return its State-supplied weapons.

Illinois justice was unable to convict the killers of Joseph Smith and his brother, and anti-Mormon mobs burned barns and crops on farms around Nauvoo. Young realized that they would have to abandon Nauvoo and settle in a frontier sanctuary. Texas was considered a possible site, as were California, Oregon, and the Island of Vancouver. Young ruled out the latter two because they were involved in ongoing boundary disputes between the United States and Great Britain. He favored the Great Basin of Utah because it was remote and virtually uninhabited by whites.

In February 1846, the main body left Nauvoo. Young organized twenty-four companies of 100 each and personally selected the leader of each company. Mormons sold most of their property for a fraction of its value. Before leaving Nauvoo, Young was continually threatened with arrest. The Mormons' trek to the West was the largest and best-organized of all migrations.

They spent the first winter on Potawatomi Indian lands just

north of Omaha, Nebraska. Young supervised the building of 538 log houses and 83 sod houses for 3,483 people. In early 1847, he assumed personal responsibility for the pilot company of 159 pioneers, seventy-two wagons, sixty-six oxen, and ninety-two horses. The company, whose goal was to chart the path to the Great Salt Lake Valley for others to follow, used artificial horizons, a circle of reflection, and sextants.

Initially, they traveled the Oregon Trail along the Platt River. They averaged ten miles a day. On the trail, they encountered hostile Pawnees and friendly Sioux Indians. On July 7, 1847, they reached Fort Bridger on the Green River. John C. Fremont's description of the Great Salt Lake Region was favorable; however, Jim Bridger, the famous scout, told them that the Indians in the area were unfriendly, and that the area's cold nights would prevent the growth of crops. When they got within fifty miles of the Great Salt Lake (near Ogden, Utah), another scout gave them a favorable report of their destination, including its agricultural potential.

On July 24, 1847, Young saw the Great Salt Lake Valley for the first time, from the mouth of Emigration Canyon, and said, "This is the place." Compared with Nauvoo, the Salt Lake Valley was dry and remote. It was forty miles long from north to south and twenty-five miles wide and bounded by majestic snow-capped mountains. Young laid out the city with streets eight rods wide in a perfect grid.

During the winter of 1847-48, Young reorganized the First Presidency of the Church and appointed Heber Kimball First Counselor. Also, he assumed the designation of prophet, seer, and revelator that had been held by Joseph Smith. By the spring of 1848, the settlement had grown from 300 to over 5,000 people.

The first crop was severely reduced by an invasion of crickets, which the settlers could not get rid of. Their prayers were answered when seagulls came from the Great Salt Lake to consume them. Mormons benefited economically during 1849, when wagonloads of gold prospectors passed through on their way to California. Mormons repaired the travelers' harnesses and wagons and sold supplies to them.

During 1849 and 1850, Young sought statehood for Utah and sent two representatives to Washington, D.C., to lobby for it. He did not want territorial status because it would involve federal observers that could limit his control. President Taylor denied the request for statehood; however, upon Taylor's death, President Fillmore granted territorial status to Utah, which was named for the Ute Indians in the region. Young was chosen as Utah's first Territorial Governor, and Mormons were appointed as Associate Justice of the Territory's Supreme Court, U.S. Marshal, and U.S. Attorney.

Young counseled keeping on friendly terms with the Ute Indians in the area. He asked Mormons to "feed them and clothe them . . . never turn them away hungry" and "teach them the art of husbandry." In his opinion, "It was cheaper to feed the Indians than to fight them." From 1850 to 1855, the number of Mormons in the Salt Lake Basin grew from 5,000 to 60,000, mainly from the East but including 15,000 from Great Britain.

In May 1857, President Buchanan sent 2,500 federal troops to Utah to remove Young as Territorial Governor. As had occurred earlier, anti-Mormon sentiment was rampant, principally due to their practice of polygamy. The original commander of federal troops was replaced by Colonel Albert Sidney Johnston, who later distinguished himself as a Confederate General during the Civil War.

Young accepted President Buchanan's appointed Governor, Alfred Cumming, but refused to let Colonel Johnston's men enter Salt Lake City. Young threatened to burn every structure built by the Mormons if the army entered the city. The Mormons vacated the city until July 1858, when peace was made with the federal government. The settlement continued to expand. Young was a good businessman and by the late 1850s had an accumulated wealth between $200,000 and $250,000, earned from lumbering, lumber mills, real estate, and a tannery.

On August 23, 1877, Young became very ill and was diagnosed with cholera. His condition worsened, and he died on August 27 exclaiming "Joseph! Joseph! Joseph!" John Taylor, senior member of the Council of Twelve, became President of the Church in 1880.

Brigham Young provided leadership for the Mormon Church at a critical period in its history, enabling it to become the largest religion founded in the United States. Also, he contributed heavily to the growth of the American frontier and is considered one of the great colonizers in the history of the United States.

NELSON MANDELA—First African President of the Union of South Africa

"During my lifetime, I have dedicated myself to this struggle of the African People. I have fought against white domination, and I have fought against black domination. I have cherished the ideal of a democratic and free society in which all persons live together in harmony and with equal opportunities. It is an ideal which I hope to live for and to achieve. But if needs be, it is an ideal for which I am prepared to die."

Nelson Mandela

Nelson Mandela spent over twenty-seven years in the Union of South Africa's prisons for political activism in striving to eliminate racial segregation and to improve the living and working conditions of the blacks of South Africa. In February 1990, he was released from prison and was overwhelmed by the fervor with which he was greeted by the people.

In April 1994, for the first time in the history of South Africa, black people voted to elect leaders of their choice. On May 19, 1994, Nelson Mandela was inaugurated as the first black President of the Union of South Africa.

Nelson Rolihlahla Mandela was born on July 18, 1918, at Qunu in the Transkei reserve on the east coast of South Africa. He was the eldest son of Henry and Nonqaphi Mandela, members of the royal family of the Thembu, a Xhosa-speaking people. His Xhosa name, Rolihlahla means "stirring up trouble." Henry Mandela was the chief councilor to the leader of the Thembu people and served on the Transkeian Territories General Council.

Young Nelson worked on the family farm plowing the fields and tending the cattle and sheep. He attended the local school run by white missionaries. When he was twelve, Henry Mandela became ill and sent his son to live with the Chief of the Thembu. Nelson was raised with the Chief's son and attended the Methodist High School.

In 1936, Mandela enrolled in Fort Hare College, a Methodist college in eastern Cape Province. At Fort Hare, he met many future activist leaders, including Oliver Tambo, who later became the leader of the African National Congress. Mandela's political leanings took shape in college. After three years of college, he was suspended for boycotting the Students' Representative Council, of which he was a member, because the college administration had reduced the powers of the council.

Mandela returned to the Transkei. The Chief was disappointed in him; he encouraged him to cooperate with the college administration. Mandela moved to Johannesburg, the center of the gold-mining region in the Transvaal, to avoid the arranged marriage that the Chief had planned for him.

Cosmopolitan Johannesburg was a shock to Mandela, who was used to rural and small-town life. Like all "Bantus," the white name for black Africans, he lived in a township on the outskirts of the city with no electricity or sewers. Initially, he worked as a guard at a mining compound. He had to carry a government-issued pass at all times. In the township of Alexandra, he met Walter Sisulu, owner of a real estate agency, who loaned him money to complete his college degree.

Sisulu also helped Mandela find a job with a Johannesburg law firm to finance his law studies at the University of Witwatersrand. While studying for a law degree, he met a young nurse, Evelyn Mase, whom he married. They lived in Soweto (Southwest Townships) in Orlando Township. Sisulu, a member of the African National Congress (ANC), suggested to Mandela that he join their organization, which had been formed by journalists, lawyers, teachers, and tribal chiefs to work to end segregation. They wanted to be able to buy property and to be elected to parliament.

In 1943, Mandela joined the Youth League of the ANC. The Youth League planned to push the ANC to fight white domination by participating in protests against the white government and by spurring blacks into militant action. In September 1944, Anton Lembede was elected president of the ANC, and Mandela, Sisulu, and Tambo (Mandela's friend from college), were appointed to the executive committee.

The ANC stated their philosophy: "The Congress must be the brains-trust and power-station of the spirit of African nationalism; the spirit of African self-determination; the spirit so discernible in the thinking of our youth. It must be an organization where young African men and women will meet and exchange ideas in an atmosphere pervaded by a common hatred of oppression."

In 1946, black African mine workers held a strike for better wages in which 70,000 workers participated. Seven mines were shut down; the country's booming economy was slowed. The government reacted violently. Police, aided by army units, cut off all food and water to workers' living quarters, arrested the leaders of the strike, and used batons to beat protesters who would not return to work. After some workers were killed, the strike was broken within a week. The ANC learned lessons from the strike. They realized that in numbers alone they had the power to make social change happen. Mandela said, "We have a powerful ideology capable of capturing the masses. Our duty is now to carry that ideology fully to them."

In 1949 at the ANC annual conference, the Youth League implemented a new policy of action employing strikes, civil disobedience, and noncooperation. They were convinced that they had to become more militant and had to use mass action to fight apartheid, the government's program of racial separation and white supremacy. In 1950, the ANC became allied with the Indian National Congress in South Africa, which was better financed than the ANC. Mandela learned about the passive resistance campaigns waged by Mohandas Gandhi in Africa earlier in the twentieth century. He respected the Indians' hard work and dedication to their cause, but he felt that the African movement should be separate. The Indian National Congress worked closely with the South African Communist Party. Mandela noted, "It is clear that the exotic plant of communism cannot flourish on African soil."

Also in 1950, Mandela completed his law studies and set up a a law practice in Johannesburg with Oliver Tambo. Most of their cases involved victims of apartheid laws. Tambo observed: "South African apartheid laws turn innumerable innocent people into 'criminals.' Every case in court, every visit to the prison to interview clients, reminded us of the humiliation and suffering burning into our people."

On May 1, 1950, the ANC scheduled a one-day national work stoppage. Over half of native South African workers stayed home. The strike was successful; however, nineteen Africans were killed in Johannesburg when police attacked demonstrators. Mandela commented: "That day was a turning point in my life, both in understanding through firsthand experience the ruthlessness of the police, and in being deeply impressed by the support African work-ers had given to the May Day call."

In 1951, as newly elected national president of the Youth League, Mandela was asked to lead a Defiance Campaign. He toured the country to sign up volunteers. In June 1952 in Port Elizabeth, the Defiance Campaign began their "defiance" by singing African freedom songs, calling out freedom slogans, and using the "Europeans only" entrances to post offices and railroad stations.

In Johannesburg, Sisulu, Mandela, and fifty Defiance Campaign volunteers were arrested for violating the 11:00 p.m. curfew. A volunteer broke his ankle when a guard pushed him down a flight of stairs; he was then refused medical attention. When Mandela protested to the policeman, he was beaten with a night-stick. By the end of December 1952, over 8,000 Defiance Campaign volunteers had been arrested.

Mandela and other ANC leaders were tried in December 1952. Mandela and over fifty of the ANC's most capable leaders were prohibited from participating further in the organization. Mandela was forbidden to travel outside of Johannesburg for two years, and he was not permitted to attend political meetings. By year-end 1952, ANC membership had grown to 100,000.

Mandela was away from home most of the time, putting con-siderable strain on his marriage. Evelyn was raising their children by herself, and, with his commitment to the ANC, she could fore-see no improvement in their relationship. He was never out of the view of undercover police. She moved with the children to Natal. Finally, Mandela and Evelyn were divorced.

On December 5, 1956, 156 people, including Mandela, Sisulu, and Tambo, were arrested and charged with treason as members of "a countrywide conspiracy, inspired by communism, to overthrow the State by violence." The "Treason Trial" lasted for six years, during which time Mandela, who helped to prepare the defense, was alternately in jail and out on bail. During one of the times that he was out of jail, Mandela was introduced to Winnie Nomzamo Madikizela by Oliver Tambo and his fiancée, Adelaide Tsukudu.

Winnie's Xhosa name, Nomzamo, means "she who strives." Winnie, whose parents were both teachers, graduated from Shawbury High School and enrolled in the Jan Hofsmeyr School of

Social Work in Johannesburg. Upon graduating with honors from the Hofsmeyr School, she won a scholarship to study for an advanced degree in sociology in the United States. Instead, she accepted a position at the Baragwanath Hospital in Soweto and became the first black medical social worker in South Africa.

Mandela was thirty-eight years old when he met Winnie. She was nervous because he was a national figure sixteen years older than she was. A white resident of Cape Town at the time observed: "I noticed people were turning and staring at the opposite pavement and I saw this magnificent figure of a man, immaculately dressed. Not just blacks, but whites were turning to admire him." While they were dating, Winnie commented: "Life with him was a life without him. He did not even pretend that I would have a special claim on his time."

In June 1958, Mandela and Winnie were married in the Methodist church in Bizana, Pondoland. They moved into a home in the Orlando West township of Soweto. Winnie joined the ANC and enrolled in a course in public speaking. Soon after their marriage, they were awakened in the middle of the night by security police who searched their home but found nothing incriminating.

At a mass demonstration organized by the Women's League of the ANC, Winnie and 1,200 other female protesters were arrested and imprisoned. Winnie, who was pregnant, was struck several times and almost lost her baby. Upon her release from prison, Winnie was told that she had been fired from her position at the hospital. She found a job with the Child Welfare Society.

In 1959, a militant group split off from the ANC because they did not want to cooperate with other racial groups; they advocated "Africa for Africans" and called themselves the Pan Africanist Congress (PAC). In the following year, the PAC planned a campaign against the requirement for all blacks to carry a pass.

On March 21, 1960, in Sharpeville, 10,000 protesters gathered in peaceful support of the ban on passes. The police panicked and fired into the unarmed crowd, killing sixty-seven Africans, including eight women and ten small children. Most were shot in the back as they were running away.

Later, the police fired into a peaceful crowd in the township of Langa, outside of Cape Town, killing fourteen and wounding many others. The government of the Union of South Africa was universally condemned by world opinion. The United Nations Security Council spoke out against the government of the Union of South Africa for the first time. The ANC decided to send one of their leaders outside of the country, beyond the jurisdiction of the police of South Africa. Oliver Tambo was chosen to go.

In March 1961, the chief judge announced a verdict of not guilty in the treason trial. Spectators cheered and shouted "Nkosi Sikelel' iAfrika" (God Bless Africa). Mandela had conducted the defense, cross-examined witnesses, and given testimony himself. He emphasized that the ANC through their Defiance Campaign had conducted nonviolent activities and maintained that, in the long run, civil disobedience would free all Africans. His defense brought him an international reputation and increased his standing within the ANC; he was now considered its strongest leader.

Mandela had responded to the accusation that the freedom of the ANC was a threat to Europeans (whites): "No, it is not a direct threat to the Europeans. We are not non-white; we are against white supremacy and in struggling against white supremacy we have the support of some sections of the European population. We said that the campaign we were about to launch was not directed at any racial group. It was directed against laws we considered unjust."

After spending a brief time with his family, Mandela went on the road. His first stop was the All-in-Africa Conference in Pietermaritzburg, where he was the keynote speaker. He was elected head of the National Action Council. He decided to go underground to plan further protests.

Mandela became known as the "black pimpernel," modeled on the fictional English character who always eluded his enemies during the French Revolution. He stayed underground for a year and a half, surfacing only for meetings. On one occasion, he had to climb down a rope from an upstairs window in the back of a house while police entered the front.

Winnie would be given a message to meet someone in a car at a certain location. She would change cars frequently: "By the time I reached him I had gone through something like ten cars. The people who arranged this were mostly whites. I don't know to this day who they were. I would just find myself at the end of the journey in some white house; in most cases when we got there they were deserted."

One day at work, Winnie was told to drive to a particular corner of the city. She described the incident: "When I got there, a tall man in blue overalls and a chauffeur's white coat and peaked hat opened the door, ordered me to shift from the driver's seat and took over and drove. That was him. He had a lot of disguises and he looked so different that for a moment, when he walked toward the car, I didn't recognize him myself."

By June 1961, the ANC realized that the tactic of nonviolence had failed. They were going to have to "answer violence with violence." A new organization was formed, the Umkhonto we Sizwe (Spear of the Nation, or MK), to conduct violent attacks against the government. The MK was not a terrorist organization; they limited their attacks to sabotage, mainly of power plants, railroad freight cars, and transmission lines where innocent bystanders wouldn't be injured. If caught, MK saboteurs faced the death penalty. The police stepped up their search for Mandela.

In January 1962, Mandela traveled out of South Africa for the first time. Oliver Tambo asked him to speak at the Pan African Freedom Conference in Addis Ababa, Ethiopia. For leaving the country without a passport, Mandela was charged with an additional "crime." He was moved by the open environment outside of South Africa: "Free from white oppression, from the idiocy of apartheid and racial arrogance, from police molestation, from humiliation and indignity. Wherever I went, I was treated like a human being."

Mandela returned to South Africa. On August 5, 1962, he was captured returning to Johannesburg from a meeting in Natal as the result of a tip by an informer. He was accused of inciting a strike in 1961 and of leaving the country illegally. At his trial in Pretoria, Mandela shouted to the gallery, "Amandla!" (power), and the crowd in the gallery answered "Ngawethu!" (to the people).

Mandela told the court: "I consider myself neither legally nor morally bound to obey laws made by a parliament in which I have no representation. In a political trial such as this one, which involves a clash of the aspirations of the African people and those of whites, the country's courts, as presently constituted, cannot be impartial and fair." He was found guilty on both charges and sentenced to ten years of hard labor. He was imprisoned in Pretoria, where he sewed mailbags, and then transferred to the maximum-security prison on Robben Island in the Atlantic Ocean, seven miles off Cape Town.

On July 12, 1963, the police raided the ANC's Rivonia farm and captured Walter Sisulu. They found many ANC documents, including Mandela's diary of his tour of Africa and incriminating evidence that documented his role in the MK violence. On trial, he stated to the court: "I do not deny that I planned sabotage. I did not plan it in a spirit of recklessness, nor because I have any love of violence. I planned it as a result of a calm and sober assessment of the political situation that had arisen after many years of tyranny, exploitation, and oppression of my people by the whites."

On June 11, 1964, Mandela was sentenced to life imprisonment. A staff writer for the New York *Times* wrote, "To most of the world, the Rivonia defendants are heroes and freedom fighters, the George Washingtons and Ben Franklins of South Africa." The London *Times* adds, "The verdict of history will be that the ultimate guilty party is the government in power."

On Robben Island, Mandela had a small cell without electricity or sanitary facilities. It was furnished with a mat, a bedroll, two light blankets, and a bucket. He was issued cotton shorts, a khaki shirt, and a light jacket. The guards told him that he was going to die there. He rejected the offer of a special diet and did not use his international reputation to obtain special privileges. All prisoners at Robben Island considered him their leader and spokesperson. He worked in a limestone quarry, chained to another prisoner.

Every six months, prisoners were permitted one half-hour visit and were allowed to mail one letter of 500 words and to receive one letter. On Winnie's first visit, she was instructed that they could not speak in the Xhosa language, and that political subjects could not be discussed. She could not bring any presents, and their daughters could not visit their father until they were fourteen. They communicated with microphones and headsets through a glass partition that gave a distorted view of the other party.

Winnie was forced to leave her job at the Child Welfare Society. To support her family, she worked at menial jobs—in a dry cleaners, a furniture store, and a laundry—but lost the jobs when the security police threatened the owners with reprisals. Spies and informers were everywhere she went, and the police maintained an ongoing program of harassment.

The children suffered. Winnie was frequently in jail, and friends and neighbors had to care for the young girls. On one occasion, she spent seventeen months in jail; the first five months were spent in solitary confinement in filthy living conditions. This treatment made her a stronger person. Finally, she sent their daughters to Swaziland to attend school. She lived on the charity of her friends and her supporters.

On June 16, 1976, during a mass protest in Soweto, the cruelty of the government was again displayed. A Soweto leader observed:

> I saw a stream of schoolchildren marching past my house. They had just reached the Orlando West school when the police tried to stop them marching any further. The children kept on walking so the police released dogs. Then the police panicked and fired into the mass of children. I will never forget the bravery of those children. They were carrying [trashcan] lids to protect themselves and deflect the bullets. The police had dogs and tear gas and batons, but they chose instead to use bullets against those unarmed kids. The saddest sight anyone can see is a dying child crippled by bullets.

The people of Soweto responded with an uprising. Over 1,000 protesters died, and over 4,000 were wounded. Across South Africa, over 13,000 were arrested, 5,000 of whom were under eighteen. The government of the Union of South Africa was condemned in world news. The government did not respond to international opinion. In September 1977, Steve Biko, the leader of the Black Consciousness Movement died in jail from beatings and torture.

In May 1977, Winnie Mandela was banished to Brandfort in the Orange Free State, where she lived for ten years, in an attempt to minimize her role as a national leader. She was moved into a three-room concrete-block house without running water, electricity, or a sewer system. It had a dirt floor; access was by openings in the front and side walls that could not be closed. Communication was difficult. Local people spoke only the African languages, Sotho and Tswana; Winnie spoke English and Xhosa. In communicating with the outside world, Winnie began to use the international press.

Winnie received an honorary doctor of laws degree from Haverford College, and two Scandinavian newspapers awarded her the Freedom Prize. In January 1985, U.S. Senator Edward Kennedy visited Winnie at Brandfort while on a trip to South Africa.

While Winnie was receiving international attention, Nelson Mandela continued to lead even while in prison. The United Democratic Front stated their opinion: "You [Nelson Mandela] are a true leader of the people. We will not rest until you are free. Your release and the release of all political prisoners is imperative. Your sacrifice for your people is affirmed. We commit ourselves anew to a free South Africa in which the people shall govern." Bishop Desmond Tuto said, "The government has to come to terms with the fact that the black community now says, 'Our leader is Nelson Mandela and any other persons are just filling in.'"

The government offered to release Mandela if he would reject violence unconditionally. He responded, "Only free men can negotiate. Prisoners cannot enter into contracts. I cannot and will not give any undertaking at a time when I and you, the people, are not free. Your freedom and mine cannot be separated. I will return."

In 1985, British Conservative Lord Bethell described Mandela upon visiting him in prison:

> A tall, lean figure with silvering hair, an impeccable olive-green shirt and well-creased navy blue trousers. He could almost have seemed like another general in the South African prison service. Indeed his manner was the most self-assured of them all, and he stood out as obviously the senior man in the room.

> He was, however, black. And he was a prisoner, perhaps the most famous in the world, the man they write songs about in Europe and name streets after in London, the leader of the African National Congress, a body dedicated to the destruction of the apartheid system, if necessary by force.

Samuel Dash, chief counsel for the U.S. Senate Watergate Committee, observed on a visit that the guards treated Mandela "as though he were their superior, unlocking gates and opening doors on his command as he led me on a tour of his building." When Dash commented on the whites' fear of the black majority, Mandela pointed out that "unlike white people anywhere else in Africa, whites in South Africa belong here—this is their home. We want them to live here with us and to share power with us."

Dash noted: "I felt that I was in the presence not of a guerrilla fighter or radical ideologue, but of a Head of State." Mandela reiterated the principles of the ANC to Dash:

- A unified South Africa without artificial "homelands"
- Black representation in the central parliament
- One man, one vote

On February 11, 1990, Nelson Mandela was released from prison. His first speech to the people was given in Cape Town at the Grand Parade, a large square in front of the old City Hall.

Mandela greeted the reception committee and the huge crowd. "Friends, comrades, and fellow South Africans. I greet you all in the name of peace, democracy, and freedom for all! I stand here before you not as a prophet but as a humble servant of you, the people. Your tireless and heroic sacrifices have made it possible for me to be here today. I therefore place the remaining years of my life in your hands."

In late February, Mandela traveled to Lusaka to attend a meeting of the National Executive Committee of the ANC. He enjoyed being reunited with comrades that he hadn't seen in many years. He also spoke with heads of state of other African countries, including Angola, Botswana, Mozambique, Uganda, Zambia, and Zimbabwe. After the conference, Mandela traveled around Africa and visited the Egyptian president, Hosni Mubarak, in Cairo. While in Egypt, Mandela stated at a press conference that the ANC was "prepared to consider a cessation of hostilities." This was a message for the government of South Africa.

Upon Mandela's return to South Africa, the ANC leadership, including Mandela and Walter Sisulu, met with government officials in a first round of talks to discuss their differences. In early June, Mandela went on a six-week trip to Europe and North America. He met with world leaders in France, Switzerland, Italy,

Ireland, and England as well as the United States and Canada. After visiting Memphis and Boston, he traveled to Washington and addressed a joint session of Congress.

Upon his return to South Africa, Mandela realized that violence was continuing to obstruct the peace process. He traveled around the country in an attempt to soothe some of the ill feelings. On December 20, 1991, the first serious negotiations, called the Convention for a Democratic South Africa (CODESA), started between the ANC, other South African parties, and the government.

On June 3, 1993, negotiations resulted in setting a date for the first non-racial, one-person-one-vote national election in South Africa on April 27, 1994. For the first time in the history of South Africa, black voters could elect the leaders of their choice. In 1993, Mandela and President de Klerk shared the Nobel Peace Prize. Mandela accepted the prize on behalf of the people of South Africa. He acknowledged that Mr. de Klerk had made a serious, vital contribution to the peace process.

Mandela and de Klerk had one television debate before the presidential election. In his remarks, Mandela looked at de Klerk and said, "Sir, you are one of those I rely upon. We are going to face the problems of this country together." Mandela extended his hand to de Klerk and added, "I am proud to hold your hand for us to go forward." The gesture surprised de Klerk, but he agreed to work together.

Mandela won the election with 62.6 percent of the vote. He realized that now he would have to heal the country's wounds, to promote reconciliation, and to instill confidence in the leadership of the government. At his inauguration, Mandela declared:

> We have, at last, achieved our political emancipation. We pledge ourselves to liberate all our people from the continuing bondage of poverty, deprivation, suffering, gender, and other discrimination. Never, never, and never again shall it be that this beautiful land will again experience the oppression of one by another. The sun shall never set on so glorious an achievement. Let freedom reign. God bless Africa.

After his swearing-in ceremony, the ranking generals of the South African Defense Force and the security police saluted the new President and affirmed their loyalty as jet fighters, multi-engine aircraft, and helicopters of the South African Air Force flew overhead. Ceremonies were concluded with blacks singing "Die Stem van Suid-Afrika," the anthem of the republic, and whites singing "Nkosi Sikelel' iAfrica."

In *Long Walk to Freedom*, Nelson Mandela wrote:

> I have walked that long road to Freedom. I have tried not to falter; I have made missteps along the way. But I have discovered the secret that after climbing a great hill, one only finds that there are many more hills to climb. I have taken a moment to rest, to steal a view of the glorious vista that surrounds me, to look back on the distance I have come. But I can rest only for a moment, for with freedom comes responsibilities, and I dare not linger, for my long walk is not yet ended.

* * *

Brigham Young and Nelson Mandela were optimistic leaders who persevered to meet their goals. They certainly displayed the trait of emotional control: Young in dealing with the residents and local governments in Ohio and in Missouri where Mormon property was destroyed or confiscated and Mandela in his relationships with white leaders in South Africa with whom he would have to lead the country. We can learn from these individuals to control ourselves when we feel that we have every reason to react strongly.

CHAPTER 7

SOCIAL RESPONSIBILITY—ROLE MODELS

Ezra Cornell (1807-1874) Cornell University Benefactor

George Eastman (1854-1932) Photographic Industry Founder

"The saying of the seventeenth century English author John Donne: 'No man is an island'. . . encompasses the essence of the concept of social responsibility. We are all on earth together and our actions, or lack of them, impact a lot of people around us. We are socially responsible to the degree that we see ourselves as being part of something larger than ourselves. Socially responsible people have a sense of duty to make the world a better place in which to live."

Harvey Deutschendorf, *The Other Kind of Smart*

EZRA CORNELL—Cornell University Benefactor

"Cornell was a tough-minded idealist. He was a man of principle, which he displayed in a letter to his son in September 1840: 'Do right because it is right, for the sake of right and nothing else. Every act should be measured by that rule—is it right? Let a pure heart prompt an honest conscience to answer the question and all will be well.'"

Historian Carl Becker

Ezra Cornell, the principal benefactor of Cornell University, was born on January 11, 1807, at Westchester Landing, New York. He was the oldest of eleven children of Elijah Cornell and Eunice Barnard Cornell. In 1818, the Cornell family, who were birthright Quakers, moved to Deruyter, Onondaga County. Elijah was a potter, but hard economic times forced him to change his vocation to farming.

At the age of seventeen, Cornell built a shop for his father and a year later built a two-story house to replace the family's log cabin. In 1826, with nine dollars in his pocket, he walked thirty-three miles to Syracuse to find work as a carpenter. He built two sawmills and eventually moved to Homer, where he worked in a shop that made wool-carding machinery. He studied mechanics and technical drawing.

In April 1828, Cornell walked to Ithaca, where he worked as a mechanic at a cotton mill. A year later, he worked as a mechanic at Colonel Jeremiah Beebe's plaster and flour mills. Gypsum, also called land plaster, was brought to Ithaca on barges to be ground in mills. Gypsum, one of Ithaca's major products, was used as plaster, fertilizer, and as an ingredient of Portland cement. Cornell became the manager of Colonel Beebe's mills and was given the nickname "Plaster Cornell."

In March 1831, Cornell married Mary Ann Wood, the daughter of a farmer from nearby Etna. Since Mary Ann was an Episcopalian, he had married "out of meeting" and was excommunicated from the Society of Friends. He built a home and a new flour mill for Colonel Beebe. During the 1830s, he speculated in real estate.

The Panic of 1837 forced Colonel Beebe to sell his mills, and Cornell lost his job. He farmed on Colonel Beebe's farm, which he rented, and was a partner in a small grocery store that failed. In 1842, he obtained the rights to sell a plow that two of his neighbors had patented. During the summer of 1842, he was moderately success-ful at selling plows in Maine. While there, he made an acquaintance who was to change his life: F. O. J. Smith—Congressman, editor of the *Maine Farmer*, and entrepreneur.

Smith told Cornell that Congress had appropriated $30,000 for Professor Morse to test the practicality of laying telegraph line in a pipe between Washington and Baltimore. Smith had signed a con-tract to lay the pipe at $100 per mile and now he needed equipment that would allow him to make a profit on the job. Smith asked Cornell to design two machines for him, one to dig the trench for the pipe and a second machine to fill in the trench.

Cornell inspected a sample of the pipe to be laid and was con-fident that the job could be done with one machine, not two; the furrow would be so narrow that it would close itself. He sketched a machine that would feed wire in a flexible tube coiled on a reel into a furrow two and a half feet deep and a quarter of a inch wide. Smith agreed to pay for its construction. Cornell demonstrated the machine successfully to Professor Morse and was contracted to lay the line between Washington and Baltimore.

Cornell laid a half-mile of line a day; however, having doubts about the insulation on the wire, he built a machine to withdraw the wire from the pipe and reinsulate it. During the winter of 1843-44, he studied electricity and concluded that the line should be run above ground on glass-insulated poles. Early the next spring, he installed the line above ground in time for Morse to send his his-toric message from the chambers of the Supreme Court in Washington: "What hath God wrought." Cornell was at the receiv-ing end of the message at the Pratt Street railroad station of the Baltimore & Ohio Railroad in Baltimore.

In the spring of 1844, Cornell installed the telegraph line between Philadelphia and New York for Morse and his business associates, the Magnetic Telegraph Company. In 1844, Cornell invested $500 in the Magnetic Telegraph Company, which was half of his salary as construction chief. By July 1849, he had installed one-third of the telegraph lines in the country. He began the transi-tion from installer to owner of telegraph lines. In 1852, Cornell was elected president of the New York and Erie Telegraph Company.

By the mid-1850s, there were too many competing telegraph lines over parallel routes. Hiram Sibley proposed the combination of the short, unprofitable lines west of Buffalo into one network; then he purchased many of these lines. On April 4, 1856, the Western Union Telegraph Company was formed. Cornell, a director and the largest stockholder, proposed the name for the new company. However, he had become tired of the corporate infighting, and he played no active role in running the company. His investments continued to appreciate in value; the value of his stock in the Erie and Michigan Telegraph grew from $50,000 in 1857 to $2 million in 1865.

In 1857, Cornell purchased the DeWitt farm, which contained the hilltop overlooking Ithaca and Cayuga Lake. It had special significance for him; his first view of Ithaca, when he had walked into town as a twenty-one year old, was from this farm. He raised purebred cattle, planted fruit trees, and experimented with crops.

Cornell built a public library for Ithaca and Tompkins County. He purchased the property and personally drew the plans for the Cornell Free Library. He gave this gift to the community before philanthropy became popular.

In 1861, Cornell was elected to the State Assembly. The following year, he was appointed president of the State Agricultural Society, which automatically made him a trustee of the Ovid Agricultural College. He and the other Ovid Agricultural College trustees petitioned for a land grant after the passage of the Morrill Act, which provided each State with public lands to be used for establishing a college. People's College in Montour Falls was also competing for a land grant but was unable to raise the matching funds.

In November 1863, Cornell was elected to the State Senate, where he met fellow Senator Andrew Dickson White of Syracuse. White suggested to Cornell that he establish a new college with the land grant endowment and part of his fortune, instead of backing either the Ovid or Montour Falls sites. Cornell offered to donate his 300-acre hilltop farm, build the facilities, and endow the college with $300,000, if the land grant college were built at Ithaca. No one could match the $300,000 (later increased to $500,000), and Ithaca was chosen as the site of the land grant college for New York State.

Cornell and White shared the planning for Cornell University; Cornell concentrated on building and financial issues, and White was responsible for academic matters. One of White's early accomplishments was convincing Cornell to consider classics and humanities with the same importance as agriculture and mechanics, which were Cornell's principal interests. White was unanimously elected the first president of the university.

On October 8, 1868, the university opened with 412 students (332 freshmen and 80 upperclassmen). This began the fulfillment of the motto on Cornell University's Great Seal: "I would found an institution where any person can find instruction in any study." The early years were turbulent, but controlled. Discussion centered on the nonsecular nature of the college, the absence of religion courses, and the election of a layman as president. The nonsectarian aspect of university was important to the founders, who specified that: "the Board of Trustees shall be so constituted that at no time shall a majority thereof be of one religious sect, or of no religious sect."

Cornell was a moral, strong-willed individual who was molded by his early Quaker upbringing. He died in Ithaca on December 9, 1874. Historian James Anthony Froude, who met Cornell while visiting the United States, observed: "Mr. Cornell would be a sublime figure anywhere; he seems to me the most surprising and venerable object I have seen in America."

GEORGE EASTMAN—Founder of the Photographic Industry

Eastman's explanation of the origin of the word "Kodak." (He liked the letter K, the first letter of his mother's maiden name):

First: It is short.
Second: It is not capable of mispronunciation.
Third: It does not resemble anything in the art and cannot be associated with anything in the art except the "Kodak."

George Eastman was born in Waterville, New York, on July 12, 1854. He was the third child and first son of George W. Eastman and Maria Kilbourn Eastman. In 1842, Eastman's father established a business school, Eastman's Commercial College, in Rochester. The school prospered in the thriving Erie Canal community, but George W. Eastman didn't move his family from Waterville to Rochester until 1860.

George W. Eastman died in 1862, leaving the family in reduced economic circumstances. Maria Eastman had to take in boarders to supplement her meager income. Young Eastman's first job was a part-time job with an insurance agency. He started his first full-time job as junior bookkeeper for the Rochester Savings Bank in 1874.

The first reference to photography in Eastman's diary was in 1869. His interest began in earnest during the summer of 1877; he purchased $100 worth of "sundries and lenses," and arranged for a local photographer to teach him "the art of photography."

Taking photographs in 1877 was a complex process requiring a considerable amount of equipment. The glass plates had to be exposed in the camera while the emulsion was wet, and development had to be completed before the emulsion dried. Eastman was bothered by the cumbersomeness of the process. He observed, "the bulk of the paraphernalia worried me. It seemed that one ought to be able to carry less than a pack-horse load."

Eastman's thinking was given direction when he read an article in the *British Journal of Photography* that provided a formula for a sensitive gelatin emulsion for glass plates that could be used when dry. He spent long hours experimenting until he found a combination of gelatin and silver bromide that had the photographic qualities that he sought. Initially, he experimented to support his hobby of photography, but he soon realized the commercial potential of his effort. He resigned his job at the bank and began to make and market dry plates.

By June 1879, Eastman was manufacturing quality photographic plates and had designed and built equipment for coating them. He sailed to England, the center of the photographic industry, and obtained his first patent on July 22, 1879. On September 9, 1879, his patent attorney, George Selden, submitted an application for him to the U.S. Patent Office for "an Improved Process of Preparing Gelatin Dry Plates for Use in Photography and in Apparatus therefor."

In April 1880, Eastman leased the third floor of a building on State Street in Rochester and began to produce dry plates in quantity. One of the early investors in the Eastman Dry Plate Company was Colonel Henry Strong, who boarded with Maria Eastman. Strong was a partner in Strong-Woodbury and Company, a successful manufacturer of whips.

During the winter of 1879-80, Eastman formulated four business principles upon which to build his enterprise:

- Production in large quantities by machinery

- Low prices to increase the usefulness of the products

- Foreign as well as domestic distribution

- Extensive advertising as well as selling by demonstration

In 1881, a near-fatal catastrophe struck the business: photographers complained that Eastman dry plates were no longer sensitive and did not capture an image. Customers discovered something that wasn't realized until then: passage of time lessened the sensitivity of the emulsion on the plate. The New York City distributor had placed the recently received plates on top of the older plates and had sold the new plates before using up the old. By the time the older plates were sold, they had lost their photographic sensitivity. At significant expense for a small company, Eastman recalled all of his plates and replaced them.

Then Eastman received a second staggering blow: he could no

longer make a satisfactory emulsion. During many weeks of sleepless nights with his factory shut down, Eastman conducted 469 unsuccessful experiments to produce a usable emulsion. On March 11, 1882, Eastman and Strong sailed for England. In England, they discovered that the problem was due to a defective supply of gelatin received from a manufacturer; it wasn't a problem with the emulsion formula or Eastman's equipment. On April 16, they returned to Rochester, conducted sixteen more unsuccessful experiments and were successful on the seventeenth try. Eastman learned two lessons from this experience: to test samples of material received and to control the supply, whenever practical.

Eastman searched for a material to replace the fragile, heavy glass as a support for the emulsion. He experimented with collodion, which was made from gun-cotton (nitro-cellulose) and nitric acid. On March 4, 1884, he filed his first patent application for photographic film. Then he worked on a mechanism to hold film in the camera; he designed a roll-holder in a wooden frame. On October 1, 1882, the Eastman Dry Plate and Film Company was incorporated with $200,000 capital stock. Henry Strong was president, and Eastman was treasurer of the new company, which purchased the plant and stock of the Eastman Dry Plate Company. On March 26, 1885, the first commercial film was made by the new company.

Eastman used Dr. Samuel Lattimore, head of the department of chemistry at the University of Rochester, as a consultant. The first chemist hired by Eastman was Henry Reichenbach, one of Dr. Lattimore's assistants. Eastman was too involved with the operation of the business to devote much time to experiments; however, he continued to work on mechanical developments, such as roller mechanisms. On December 10, 1889, a patent for manufacturing transparent nitro-cellulose photographic film was granted to Reichenbach. Joint patents were granted to Eastman and Reichenbach on March 22, 1892, and July 19, 1892.

Another early setback to the company was a serious fire on February 10, 1888, that destroyed most of the interior of the State Street factory and shut it down for two months. Eastman was back in business in April, and by June he had his first camera on the market. He conceived of the name "Kodak" as a trademark for his products. On September 4, 1888, "Kodak" was registered as a trademark in the U.S. The first camera was the "No. 1 Kodak."

The company continued to expand to meet market demand. In August 1890, it purchased several farms in the Town of Greece that were to become Kodak Park, the world's largest film manufacturing complex. Camera and film development continued as Kodak designed and made uncomplicated products that lived up to the slogan: "You press the button and we do the rest."

The next challenge that Eastman faced was one that he least expected—employee disloyalty. Reichenbach and two other employees secretly formed a rival company using the film-making formulae and processes of Eastman's company. He also found that they had made 39,400 feet of unusable film and had let 1,417 gallons of emulsion spoil. Eastman discharged them.

On November 28, 1889, the Eastman Photographic Materials Company, Ltd., was incorporated in London to represent the company in all areas of the world except the western hemisphere. In December 1889, the Eastman Company was incorporated in Rochester with $1 million capital to represent the company in the western hemisphere. On May 23, 1892, the name of the Eastman Company was changed to the Eastman Kodak Company and the capitalization was increased to $5 million.

In 1912, Eastman established the Eastman Kodak Company Research Laboratories and brought Dr. Kenneth Mees from England to serve as its head. Mees and his chief assistant, S. E. Shepard, who were both graduates of the University of London, made significant contributions to the growth of the company. Motion pictures were introduced in the early 1920s, Kodacolor film was announced in the late 1920s, and many significant film improvements followed, including Technicolor film, Kodachrome film, and the replacement of nitrate-based film with an acetate-based product.

Eastman never married; he lived alone in his mansion on East Avenue in Rochester. On March 14, 1932, George Eastman took his own life at his East Avenue home. He left a note that read: "To my friends. My work is done. Why wait? G. E." His death shocked the community.

Karl K. Compton, president of the Massachusetts Institute of Technology, wrote in the April 15, 1932, issue of *Science* magazine:

> Consider for a moment the full significance of his last words. He had invented the modern photographic plate; he had invented photographic film; he had made Kodak a household object throughout the entire world; he had created a business; he had created a great research laboratory which had strikingly fulfilled his faith in it; he had selected certain fields of education, health, and art to which he had devoted his fortune for the benefit of the entire world; he had satisfied his distinctive desires for the excitement of exploration and big game hunting; he had no close relatives; the infirmities of old age had come upon him and were about to master him. He who had always been his own master remained so to the last.

* * *

Ezra Cornell and George Eastman are prime examples of individuals who displayed social responsibility. Cornell made millions from Western Union and wanted to give part of it to society. He contributed land and money for the founding of New York State's land grant college.

Examples of Eastman's social responsibility are the founding of the Eastman School of Music at the University of Rochester and the building of the Eastman Theatre. Also, he gave over $60 million to educational institutions, including the University of Rochester, the Massachusetts Institute of Technology, Hampton Institute, and the Tuskegee Institute. In addition, he funded the Eastman Visiting Professorship at Oxford University and gave $5.5 million to establish dental clinics in Brussels, London, Paris, Rome, and Stockholm.

CHAPTER 8

MOTIVATION—ROLE MODELS

Douglas Bader (1910-1982) World War II Royal Air Force Ace

Carl Brashear (1931-   ) U.S. Navy Master Diver and Amputee

"Motivation is the word used to describe those processes that can (a) arouse and instigate behavior, (b) give direction or purpose to behavior, (c) continue to allow behavior to exist, and (d) lead to choosing or preferring a particular behavior. A motive is any condition within a person that affects his or her readiness to initiate or continue any activity or sequence of activities."

Raymond J. Wlodkowski, *Motivation in Education*

DOUGLAS BADER—World War II Royal Air Force Ace

"The nerve that never relaxes, the eye that never blanches, the thought that never wanders—these are the masters of victory."

Edmund Burke

On Monday morning, December 14, 1931, Royal Air Force pilot Douglas Bader was flying near Kenley, England, when he saw two pilots take off from the airfield. He recalled that the pilots, Phillips and Richardson, were flying to Woodley airfield near Reading to visit Phillips's brother, who was stationed there. Bader joined them on their flight.

While visiting Woodley, one of the pilots asked Bader about the aerobatics he had performed at the air show at Hendon and asked if he would do some aerobatics for them. Bader declined the request. He vividly recalled a reprimand from his commanding officer for showing off in the air and taking too many chances. Also, the Gloster Gamecock they flew at Hendon had been replaced with the more modern and faster Bulldog. However, the Bulldog was heavier than the Gamecock and wasn't as maneuverable; furthermore, it had the tendency to drop out of a roll.

When the pilots prepared to return to Kenley, Bader was again asked to perform some aerobatics. This time, he took it as a dare. As he climbed, Bader banked and turned back to the airfield to make a low pass at the clubhouse. He rolled to the right and felt the Bulldog begin to drop. He attempted to come out of the roll when the left wingtip hit the ground. His plane crashed, and the engine was separated from the fuselage.

Bader was pinned in the aircraft by his straps. He heard the loud noise of the crash, but didn't feel much pain; however, he noticed that his legs were in unusual positions. His left leg was buckled under the seat, and he could see a bone sticking out of the right knee of his coveralls and a spreading stain of blood. His first thought was that he wouldn't be able to play rugby on Saturday.

A steward came over from the clubhouse with a glass of brandy and offered it to him. Without thinking, Bader said, "No, thanks very much. I don't drink." The steward leaned over, saw all of the blood in the cockpit, became very pale, and drank the brandy himself. The plane had to be cut away with a hacksaw before Bader could be lifted from the wreckage. He was taken to the Royal Berkshire Hospital, where both legs were amputated.

Bader was fitted for artificial legs by the Dessouter brothers at Roehampton Hospital. Robert Dessouter fitted him for the artificial legs and told him that he would never walk without a cane. Bader told him that he would never walk *with* a cane.

After many tries on the first day with the new legs, Bader hobbled a few steps, unaided, to the parallel bars. Dessouter had never seen an individual with one artificial leg do that on the first day; it was an incredible achievement for someone with two artificial legs. While Bader practiced using his new legs, Dessouter admitted that he had never seen anyone with his tenacity and resolve.

Bader asked the garage at Kenley where he had stored his MG sports car to switch the positions of the brake and clutch pedals so he could take advantage of his stronger leg and make it easier for him to drive. When the MG was ready, a mechanic drove it to the hospital at Uxbridge where Bader was recuperating.

When Bader asked the mechanic if he had any trouble driving the car over from Kenley, the mechanic said that trouble wasn't the word for it. He kept depressing the brake pedal to shift gears and putting his foot on the clutch to stop, which was even more disconcerting. Finally, he had to drive with his legs crossed, or he would never have made it. Bader learned how to drive his MG and to dance. By the summer of 1932, he was able to fly an airplane again. He applied for flight status in the Royal Air Force.

Bader reported to the Central Medical Establishment at Kingsway for a physical examination. He passed but was given an A2H rating, which meant restricted flying; he wasn't allowed to fly solo. He was assigned to the Central Flying School at Wittering for their evaluation of his abilities.

Bader's training went well at Wittering; he was confident that he would be reinstated as a pilot. He reported back to the Central Medical Establishment at Kingsway to see the Wing Commander, who acknowledged that the Central Flying School had given him a favorable report; however, he said, "Unfortunately, we cannot pass you for flying because there is nothing in the King's Regulations which covers your case."

After Hitler's invasion of Poland, Bader again asked to return to flight status. In early October 1939, he received a telegram requesting him to report to a selection board at Kingsway. Air Vice Marshal Halahan, his old commandant from the Royal Air Force College at Cranwell, was in charge of the board.

Bader wanted to fly; he requested General Duties (flying) and a A1B rating—full flying category. Air Vice Marshal Halahan forwarded a note to the Wing Commander responsible for making the decision: "I have known this officer since he was an officer at Cranwell under my command. He's the type we want. If he is fit, apart from his legs, I suggest you give him A1B category and leave it to the Central Flying School to assess his flying capabilities." The Wing Commander agreed, and he was in.

In November 1939, Bader returned to flying duties. Within three months, he was assigned to a squadron that flew Spitfires, which were much more advanced aircraft than the Gamecocks and Bulldogs he had flown in the early 1930s.

Initially, he was assigned to No. 12 Air Group at Duxford, Cambridgeshire, whose mission was to protect the industrial Midlands. He missed the first three weeks of the Battle of Britain because, in August 1940, most cross-Channel fighter sorties were flown from No. 11 Air Group fields in Kent, Sussex, and Essex. On August 30, Squadron Leader Bader's squadron received orders to support No. 11 Air Group in the Battle of Britain.

By the end of 1940, Bader had been awarded the Distinguished Service Order (DSO), a decoration given for leadership, as well as the Distinguished Flying Cross (DFC), for individual initiative in action. Ultimately, he received the bar, a second decoration, for each medal; he was only the third person to receive them. By August 1941, he had shot down over twenty-two enemy aircraft.

On August 9, 1941, Bader was returning from a mission over Bethune, France, when a Messerschmitt collided with his plane's tail. His artificial right leg caught on the cockpit as he jumped from the aircraft. Eventually, his leg harness broke, allowing him to open his parachute. If it had been his real right leg, he would probably have been pulled down with the aircraft. He landed in St. Omer, France, where he was captured by the Germans and taken to a hospital. The Germans found his right artificial leg and repaired it for him. Later, a spare leg was parachuted into St. Omer by the R.A.F.

As soon as he could walk, Bader formed a rope out of knotted bedsheets and escaped from the hospital with the aid of one of the nurses. Unfortunately, another nurse informed on the one who had helped him, and he was recaptured. He was moved to a prison camp where he made another escape attempt; eventually, after trying to escape a third and fourth time, he was transferred to the maximum security prison at Colditz. After three and a half years as prisoner of war, he was liberated. When he returned home, he was promoted to Group Captain.

In September 1945, Bader was asked to plan and lead the first Battle of Britain fly-past over London to celebrate the peace and to commemorate the fifth anniversary of the Battle of Britain. In 1956, Queen Elizabeth awarded him a Commander of the British Empire (CBE) in recognition of his services. In 1976, he was knighted by the Queen. Douglas Bader was sufficiently motivated to refuse to let his injuries divert him from achieving his goals and using his talents to defend his country.

CARL BRASHEAR—U.S. Navy Master Diver and Amputee.

"The Navy diver is not a fighting man.
He is a salvage expert.
If it's lost underwater, he finds it.
If it's sunk, he brings it up.
If it's in the way, he moves it.
If he's lucky, he dies two hundred feet beneath the waves,
Because that's the closest he will ever come to being a hero.
No one in their right mind would ever want the job.
Or so they say."

The Diver's Creed

Carl Brashear set a goal for himself at a young age and had the motivation to achieve that goal despite having to overcome racial discrimination as well as a major physical injury. Paul Stillwell of the U.S. Naval Institute summarized Brashear's achievements:

To become the first black master diver in the Navy, Carl Brashear used a rare combination of grit, determination, and persistence, because the obstacles in his path were formidable. His race was a handicap, as were his origin on a sharecropper's farm in rural Kentucky and the modest education he received there. But these were not his greatest challenges. He was held back by an even greater factor: in 1966, his left leg was amputated just below the knee because he was badly injured on a salvage operation.

After the amputation, the Navy sought to retire Brashear from active duty, but he refused to submit to the decision. Instead, he secretly returned to diving and produced evidence that he could excel, despite his injury. Then, in 1974, he qualified as a Master Diver, a difficult feat under any circumstances and something no black man had accomplished before. By the time of his retirement, he

117

had achieved the highest rate for Navy enlisted personnel, master chief petty officer. In addition, he had become a celebrity through his response to manifold challenges and thereby had become a real inspiration to others.

Carl Brashear was born on a farm in Tonieville, Kentucky, in January 1931, the sixth of nine children of McDonald and Gonzella Brashear. McDonald Brashear was a hard-working sharecropper with a third-grade education. Young Carl helped his father work the farm and attended a one-room, segregated school through the eighth grade. His mother, who had completed nine years of school, augmented his education with home schooling.

At the age of fourteen, Brashear decided that he wanted to be a military man, possibly a soldier. He was influenced by a brother-in-law in the Army. When he was seventeen, he went to the U.S. Army recruiting office to enlist. However, everyone yelled at him, making him so nervous that he failed the entrance examination. He was supposed to return to retake the exam, but he went to the U.S. Navy recruiting office instead. The Navy chief petty officer treated him well, so he enlisted in the Navy.

In February 1948, Brashear reported to the Great Lakes Naval Training Center for basic training and was assigned to an integrated company. He encountered no racial prejudice in boot camp; however, upon completion of his training, steward was the only assignment available to him. He was assigned as steward to an air squadron in Key West, Florida. The Naval Base in Key West was segregated at the time; opportunities for African-American personnel were limited.

At Key West, Brashear met Chief Boatswain's Mate Guy Johnson, who steered him toward a major turning point in his career. Chief Johnson arranged for Brashear to leave the steward assignment and to work for him as a beachmaster, beaching seaplanes from the Gulf of Mexico. Brashear strongly preferred his new assignment over his old one. His duties as a beachmaster required him to get along with people, to respect others, and to work with little supervision. Chief Johnson taught him basic seamanship, gave him guidance on being a good sailor, and introduced him to the qualities of leadership.

While stationed at Key West, Brashear decided that he wanted to be a diver. One day, a buoy needed repair, and a self-propelled seaplane wrecking derrick, a YSD, was brought out to repair it. A diver with a face mask and shallow-water diving apparatus went down to make the necessary repairs. Brashear watched the diver work and realized that diving was what he wanted to do. Brashear requested diving duty on his first two shipboard assignments, on the escort aircraft carriers *USS Palau* (CVE-122) and *USS Tripoli* (CVE-64). He was assigned to the sail locker, with boatswain's mate's duties such as splicing wire and sewing canvass. He learned about fueling rigs and anchoring and mooring methods.

While Brashear was stationed on the *Tripoli,* a TBM Avenger torpedo bomber rolled off the jettison ramp, and a deep-sea diver went down to attach wires to pull the plane out of the water. Brashear watched the diver go down and come up and observed, "Now, this is the best thing since sliced bread. I've got to be a deep-sea diver." He requested diving school routinely until he was admitted in 1954.

Brashear joined the boxing team on the *Tripoli* and won many bouts. He met Sugar Ray Robinson, who taught him how to throw jabs and to keep his hands up. Sugar Ray showed him how to be a better defensive boxer. Brashear fought in the light-heavyweight championship of the East Coast, but he lost that fight.

Brashear made boatswain's mate third class on the *Tripoli* and gained experience with paravane gear used for minesweeping and with the operations of a tank landing ship (LST). He was responsible for a division of men and learned about leadership and supervision. He had done well, but he realized that further education would increase his opportunities for advancement.

In 1953, Brashear made boatswain's mate second class. While at that rate, he won "sailor-of-the-year" honors and was called "Mr. Navy." He enrolled in United States Armed Forces Institute (USAFI) courses and passed his general educational development (GED) examination, the high-school equivalency test, in 1960. A high school diploma wasn't required for the first phase of diving school, but it was for later phases, such as mixed-gas diving.

Brashear's next assignment was in Bayonne, New Jersey, at diving school, which involved hard work and psychological stress. When he reported for duty, the training officer thought he was reporting in as a cook or steward. When he found out that Brashear was there as a student, he told him, "Well, I don't know how the rest of the students are going to accept you. As a matter of fact, I don't even think you will make it through the school. We haven't had a colored guy come through here before."

When classes started, Brashear found notes on his bunk: "We're going to drown you today, nigger! We don't want any nigger divers." Brashear was ready to quit, but boatswain's mate first class Rutherford, on the staff of the diving school, talked him out of it. Over a beer at the Dungaree Bar, Rutherford said, "I hear you're going to quit." Brashear admitted that he planned to leave the school. Rutherford told him, "I can't whip you, but I'll fight you every day if you quit. Those notes aren't hurting you. No one is doing a thing to you. Show them you're a better man than they are." Rutherford's pep talk was the only encouragement that Brashear received. One person's upbeat advice was enough to keep Brashear on his chosen career path.

The first week of diving school was orientation; physics courses were given in the second week. Diving medicine and diving physics were followed by four weeks of pure diving, which included introduction to hydraulics and underwater tools as well as underwater welding and cutting. The course included two weeks of demolition and several weeks of salvage operations, which involved becoming familiar with beach gear and learning how to make splices.

Brashear worked hard in the sixteen-week-long diving school and didn't fail any exams. The school was stressful; the instructors continually challenged the students. Teamwork was emphasized. When working underwater, divers rely on their teammates working alongside them and rely heavily on support personnel topside. Seventeen out of thirty-two that started with the class graduated.

In March 1955, Brashear was assigned to a salvage ship, *USS Opportune* (ARS-41), which had eighteen divers out of a crew of over 100. The *Opportune* was involved in many salvage jobs, including raising a gas barge in Charleston, South Carolina; recovering an antisubmarine plane that had sunk in the Virginia Capes; and pulling a cargo ship off the beach in Argentia, Newfoundland. His experiences on the *Opportune* increased his understanding of teamwork and the importance of knowing other team members' capabilities in diving. He was promoted to boatswain's mate first class while in Argentia, Newfoundland.

Brashear's next duty station was Quonset Point (Rhode Island) Naval Air Station, where, as leading petty officer, he was in charge of the boat house. One of his assignments was retrieving aircraft that had crashed in Narragansett Bay. A collateral duty was to escort President Eisenhower's boat, the *Barbara Ann*, with a 104-foot crash boat with a crew of thirteen and two 20-millimeter guns mounted on the wings of the bridge, from Delaware to Newport, where Ike played golf. Brashear also escorted the *Barbara Ann* on pleasure cruises.

One of Brashear's next assignments was the *USS Nereus*, homeported in San Diego, California, where he made chief petty officer and was assigned to first-class diver school in Washington, D.C. First-class diver school was demanding, with courses in medicine, decompression, physics, treatments, mathematics, and mixing gases to the proper ratio. Brashear flunked out. Most salvage divers who failed first-class school left as a second-class diver.

Brashear was astounded to hear that he was leaving as a non-diver. After seven years of diving experience, he had reached the low point in his career. He wrangled a set of orders to the fleet training center in Hawaii, which he knew had a second-class diver school. Lieutenant j.g. Billie Delanoy, whom Brashear knew from a previous assignment, was in charge of that school. Delanoy knew that his old shipmate should be a diver and enrolled him in the school, which was not difficult for Brashear. He passed it easily and returned to a level he had mastered previously.

While in Hawaii, Brashear dove to inspect the hull of the *USS Arizona* (BB-39) before she could be converted into a memorial. The amount of list had to be determined before they could proceed with the work to build the memorial. Using plumb lines, they determined that the *Arizona* had two degrees of list. It gave him an eerie feeling diving around a hull containing the 1,100 shipmates that didn't survive the Japanese attack on Pearl Harbor.

While assigned to the fleet training center in Hawaii, Brashear received temporary additional duty (TAD) to report to Joint Task Force Eight as a diver supporting nuclear testing during Operation Dominic in 1962. Thor intermediate-range ballistic missiles (IRBMs) with 20- or 30-megaton warheads were tested on

Johnston Island. Brashear was skipper of a large self-propelled harbor tug (YTB-262) and was also a diver.

After studying math for two years, in 1963 Brashear got a second opportunity to attend first-class diving school in Washington, D.C. He thought that he would go through fourteen weeks of training with the class of thirty salvage divers, learning about diving medicine, diving physics, mixing gases, and emergency procedures. However, the training officer made him go through twenty-six weeks of class as though he had never been a salvage diver. He graduated third out of seventeen who completed the course.

After serving a year on the fleet ocean tug *USS Shakori* (ATF-162), Brashear was assigned to the salvage ship *USS Hoist* (ARS-40), where he could train to become a master diver. The *Hoist* participated in the search for a nuclear bomb that was dropped into the sea off Palomares, Spain, when a B-52 bomber and a refueling plane collided in midair. The bomb was found by the deep-diving research vessel *Alvin* six miles off the coast in 2,600 feet of water after a search of two and a half months. Brashear rigged a spider, a three-legged contraption with grapnel hooks, to the bomb to bring it to the surface.

A mechanized landing craft (LCM-8) was moored alongside the *Hoist* to receive the bomb. Brashear was bringing the bomb up with the capstan to place it in a crate in the landing craft when a line parted, causing the boat to break loose. He saw what had happened and ran to push one of his men out of the way of the line. A pipe tied to the mooring came loose, sailed across the deck, and struck Brashear's left leg just below the knee, virtually severing it. The bomb fell back into 2,600 feet of water.

The *Hoist* had no doctor and no morphine and was six and a half miles from the cruiser *USS Albany,* the location of the nearest doctor. Corpsmen placed two tourniquets on his leg, but, because Brashear's leg was so muscular, the bleeding couldn't be stopped. He was placed on board a helicopter to be transported to the hospital at Torrejon Air Force Base in Spain.

Brashear had lost so much blood that he went into shock. By the time he reached Torrejon, he had hardly any heartbeat or pulse. The doctor thought that Brashear was going to die. He came to after they had given him eighteen pints of blood. He was told that they would try to save his leg, but that it would be three inches shorter than his right leg. However, his leg became infected, and gangrene set in. The doctor asked him, "Do you want to be air-lifted to the United States?" He said yes and was transported to the Portsmouth Naval Hospital in Virginia.

In Portsmouth, Brashear was told that his rehabilitation would take three years. He decided that he couldn't wait that long to get on with his life, so he told the doctor to amputate. The doctor responded, "Geez, Chief! Anybody could amputate. It takes a good doctor to fix it." Brashear told them that he planned to go back to diving; they thought that he shouldn't even consider it. In July 1966, another inch and a half of his leg had to be amputated.

Brashear had read of an air force pilot with no legs who flew fighter aircraft. That was Douglas Bader, a Royal Air Force ace in World War II. He also read that a prosthesis could be designed to support any amount of weight. He was sent to a prosthesis center in Philadelphia to be fitted. He worked around the hospital and refused to have people wait on him. Brashear told the doctor, "Once I get a leg, I'm going to give you back this crutch, and I'll never use it again." They told him that he couldn't do it. In December, he was fitted with an artificial leg; he never used crutches again.

Brashear returned to the Portsmouth Naval Hospital and visited Chief Warrant Officer Clair Axtell, who was in charge of the nearby diving school. He told Axtell, whom he knew from salvage diving school, "Ax, I've got to dive. I've got to get some pictures. I've got to prove to people that I'm going to be a diver." Axtell reminded Brashear that if anything happened to him, his own career would be over; nevertheless, he obtained a photographer and gave him a chance. Brashear dove in a deep-sea rig, in shallow-water equipment, and with scuba gear while the photographer documented his activities. He returned for a second set of dives and another set of pictures.

Brashear's medical board was convened at the naval hospital, where Rear Admiral Joseph Yon from the Bureau of Medicine and Surgery (BuMed) talked with him about returning to diving. Brashear took the initiative to endorse his own orders, "FFT (for further transfer) to the second-class diving school," and reported to the school. A lieutenant commander from BuMed called Brashear at the diving school and asked how he got into the diving school. Brashear replied, "Orders, sir," which caused some confusion.

Brashear had ignored the first physical evaluation board; now they told him to report to a second one. He had sent all of his diving photographs along with the findings of the medical board to BuMed. They said, "Well, if he did that down there [in Virginia], he can do it up here," and invited him to spend a week with a captain and a commander at the deep-sea diving school in Washington, D.C. BuMed sent observers to evaluate his performance.

At the end of the week, Captain Jacks, policy control, called Brashear in and told him: "Most of the people in your position want to get a medical disability, get out of the Navy, and do the least they can and draw as much pay as they can. And then you're asking for full duty. I don't know to handle it. Suppose you would be diving and tear your leg off." Brashear said, "Well, Captain, it wouldn't bleed." Captain Jacks jokingly told him to get out of his office.

Brashear reported back to diving school in Virginia. Brashear dove every day for a year, including weekends. He led calisthenics every morning and ran every day. Occasionally, he would return from a run and find a puddle of blood from his stump in the artificial leg. Instead of going to sick bay, he soaked his stump in a bucket of warm salt water. At the end of the year, Brashear received a very favorable report, and returned to duty with full diving assignments—the first time in naval history for an amputee.

Brashear received orders to the boat house at the Norfolk Naval Air Station, where he was a division officer in charge of the divers. Their principal duties were search and rescue and recovery of downed aircraft. They picked up helicopters and jet aircraft that had crashed and assisted civilian divers at the Norfolk Naval Shipyard.

Brashear considered becoming a warrant officer or a limited duty officer, an officer who came up from the enlisted rates. However, a Master Diver must be a chief petty officer, a senior petty officer, or a master chief petty officer, and Brashear's goal was still to be the first African-American Master Diver in the Navy.

In 1970, Brashear went from the Norfolk Naval Air Station boat house to saturation diving school at the Experimental Diving Unit in Washington, D.C. Saturation diving involves going to extreme depths and staying down for long periods of time. Upon graduation from saturation diving school, he attended master diving school. A Master Diver is proficient in all phases of diving, submarine rescue, and salvage; it is the highest position in diving.

Evaluation is done by Master Divers, ex-Master Divers, and the commanding officer and the executive officer of the Master Diving school. Emphasis is placed on emergency procedures. Considerable pressure is placed on participants, and many attempts are made to rattle them. At times, participants are given an incorrect order; they are expected to know better than to obey it. Self-confidence is a requirement. Master Divers have to know how to treat all types of diving accidents. Four out of six in the class made Master Diver, including Brashear. The commanding officer of the Master Diving school called Brashear into his office and told him, "If there was a mark that we'd give, you made the highest mark of any man that ever came through this school to be evaluated for Master. You did not make a mistake. We vote you Master."

Brashear was assigned to the submarine tender *USS Hunley* (AS-31) in Charleston, South Carolina. He was a division officer on the *Hunley*, which was a tender for nuclear submarines, both fast attack submarines and "boomers" with missiles. Divers, who were required to dive when nuclear reactors were critical, used film badges to continually check radiation levels. They had to make security checks, looking for foreign objects attached to the hull.

Brashear's next duty was on the salvage ship *USS Recovery* (ARS-43). He preferred salvage work to duty on a tender because salvage jobs were less repetitive. *Recovery* divers evaluated the feasibility of raising a ship that had sunk off Newport News in 1918 and salvaged a helicopter off the coast of Florida. They also dove in a flooded engine room on the *USS Saratoga* (CVA-60).

Recovery was a happy ship; Brashear contributed to this environment by being fair, leading by example, and by following a policy of admitting an error when one was made. Men respected him.

Brashear's next assignment was the Naval Safety Center in Norfolk, where he worked for Rear Admiral Robert Dunn. Dunn was impressed; every time his Master Diver would go out on an assignment, someone would send a bravo zulu message, a "well done," upon his return. During this assignment, Brashear headed a tiger team that conducted a field change on the Mark I dive system, including changes to the breathing mechanism and the bail-out bottle connection. Naval Sea Systems Command approved the changes, which saved the government thousands of dollars.

Brashear represented the Safety Center in investigating diving accidents, determining the cause, and making recommendations to prevent future accidents. He also conducted safety presentations and wrote "safety grams." While at the Safety Center, he was mentioned in newspapers and magazines and received television coverage. Robert Manning of the Office of the Navy's Chief of Information (Chinfo) suggested making a short movie about Brashear; a four-and-a-half minute movie was made for TV.

From that beginning, Manning suggested that Brashear should be a candidate for the "Come Back" program about people who have been injured or stumbled in their career and made a comeback. That year a thirty-minute documentary was made about Brashear as well as Rosemary Clooney, Neil Sadaka, Freddie Fender, and Bill Veeck.

Brashear's final tour of duty in the Navy was reassignment to the *USS Recovery*. The commanding Officer of the *Recovery* had requested him. Breashear considered it a feather in his cap to finish his Navy career on the *Recovery*.

Brashear retired in April 1979. His retirement ceremony was planned for the *USS Hoist*, the ship on which he had lost his leg. However, the *Hoist* was too small to accommodate everyone, so his retirement ceremony was moved to the gymnasium at the Little Creek Amphibious Base. It was announced in the newspapers three days in advance, and posters were put up all around the Amphibious Base. The gymnasium was filled; two television stations covered the event.

Brashear had the motivation to reach his goal in the Navy and enjoyed an exciting, rewarding career. In terms of his professional life, he grew up and matured in the Navy. As with many successful people, Brashear always displayed the "can do" spirit. His life is an inspiration to us.

* * *

Douglas Bader and Paul Brashear were highly motivated individuals who dealt with severe physical handicaps: Bader in overcoming the loss of both legs and Brashear overcoming the loss of one leg. Bader learned to drive a car and to play squash and golf after losing both legs in an airplane crash as well as to return to flight status as a Royal Air Force pilot. Brashear became a Master Diver, the first black Master Diver, by shear force of will. The main thing he was motivated to do with his life was to be a Master Diver in the U.S. Navy.

CHAPTER 9

ASSERTIVENESS—ROLE MODELS

Emmeline Pankhurst (1858-1928) Women's Rights Leader in England

Margaret Sanger (1883-1966) Birth Control Reformer

"Assertiveness is the ability to maintain our boundaries and express our needs clearly and directly. It includes being able to express emotions that we are feeling and offer opinions that may be unpopular or run counter to the 'group think.' Although being assertive means asking for what we want, it does not mean that we always get what we ask for. Assertiveness has gotten a bad rap in society because it is often confused with aggression."

Harvey Deutschendorf, *The Other Kind of Smart*

EMMELINE PANKHURST—Women's Rights Leader in England

"My childhood was protected by love and a comfortable home. Yet, while I was still a very young child, I began to instinctively feel that there was something lacking, even in my own home, some incomplete ideal. This vague feeling began to shape itself into conviction about the time my brothers and I were sent to school. My parents, especially my father, discussed the importance of my brothers' education as a matter of real importance. My education and that of my sister were scarcely discussed at all. A girl's education at that time seemed to have for its prime object the art of 'making the home attractive'—presumably to migratory male relatives."

Emmeline Pankhurst

Emmeline Pankhurst and her three daughters played a major role in the Women's Suffrage Movement. Emmeline, who was born in 1858, was the attractive, delicate eldest daughter of Robert Goulden, a wealthy Manchester cotton manufacturer. She was sent to finishing school in Paris.

After returning from Paris in 1878, Emmeline met Richard Pankhurst, a radical advocate who had been called to the Bar in 1867 after receiving the highest law degrees at London University. In 1865, when Emmeline was only seven years old, Pankhurst had helped found the Woman's Suffrage Society in Manchester. In 1870, he drafted the Married Women's Property Bill that gave women the right to own property and to keep the wages they earned. Also that year, he drafted the first of many parliamentary bills to give women the vote.

Emmeline and Richard fell in love at first sight. She was captivated by his "eloquence and his idealism." He was a forty-year-old bachelor who lived at home with his mother. When his mother died in 1879, he proposed to Emmeline. Theirs was a happy marriage, partly because they saw each other as kindred spirits ("Every struggling cause shall be ours").

Four children were born during the first six years of their marriage: Christabel in 1880, Sylvia in 1882, Adela in 1885, and a son who died in childhood. Pankhurst thought of his children as the pillars of his house. He told them: "If you do not grow up to help other people, you will not have been worth the upbringing." He continually counseled them that drudgery and drill are important components of life, but that "life is nothing without enthusiasms."

The subject of women's rights was Richard Pankhurst's most zealous activity and the one in which he was a strong influence on his wife and daughters. As one who opposed exploitation of all kinds, he couldn't tolerate half of the population being held back economically and politically.

In 1890, when Christabel was ten and Sylvia was eight, the usually calm Pankhurst erupted after a meeting of the Women's Franchise League at their home. He burst out, "Why don't you force us to give you the vote? Why don't you scratch our eyes out?" Christabel and Sylvia were startled by his outburst; Emmeline was astonished at the strength of his feelings.

In 1894, married women were given the right to vote in local elections and became eligible for election as district councilors and Poor Law Guardians. The following year, Emmeline was elected to the Chorlton Board of Guardians. When she was told that the Guardians couldn't provide relief to the "able bodied poor," she organized food kitchens. She was horrified by conditions in the workhouses and incensed by the treatment of young women with illegitimate babies. Years later, she wrote, "Though I had been a suffragist before, I now begin to think about the vote in women's hands not only as a right, but as a desperate necessity."

In 1895, Richard Pankhurst ran unsuccessfully for Parliament as a candidate from Gorton. The Pankhurst daughters watched helplessly as toughs threw stones at their mother while they celebrated the Tory victory. In 1896, the Manchester Parks Committee ruled that the women could no longer use Boggart Clough, a large, municipally-owned field, for their women's rights meetings as they had for several years. Speakers were fined and sent to jail unless they paid the fines. Emmeline, as the wife of a senior member of the Bar, surprised the magistrates when she told them she would pay no fine and would continue to attend meetings there. Eventually, the ban was retracted; assertiveness and controlled agitation, as well as courage and persistence had won the cause.

After the death of Lydia Decker, their dynamic leader, the suffragists in England became divided on the amount of political involvement that they should have. The leaders, who were looking for dynamic women to work in the movement, asked Christabel if she would join their cause.

Christabel was flattered and pursued her new duties with vigor. Emmeline's interest in the suffrage movement was increased by her daughter's participation. She began to work actively for the Women's Rights Movement, thereby establishing an extraordinary mother-daughter partnership.

Christabel discovered that she was a natural leader and speaker. Her intelligence, pleasant appearance, and forceful personality impressed her audiences. Christabel had an internal need to dominate her environment. The suffrage movement provided Christabel with a forum to display her strengths.

In 1903, Emmeline invited Labour Party women to a meeting at her home and founded the Women's Social and Political Union (WSPU), a name suggested by Christabel. Their motto was "Deeds, not words"; their slogan was "Votes for women." For the next eleven years, it disseminated the views of this remarkable mother-daughter partnership.

In 1905, Emmeline and Sylvia heavily lobbied the Members of Parliament to provide a place in their ballot in support of the women's cause. MP Keir Hardie was their only supporter. Finally, when MP Branford Slack, "at the request of his wife," agreed to introduce a women's suffrage bill, it was scheduled for debate on May 12.

Many women attended the debate; some came from as far away as Australia. Unfortunately, filibusters took up most of the available time, and MP Slack was allowed only a half hour. Women's suffrage had not been defeated; debate on it had merely been circumvented.

The women were upset with the government. They realized that relying on private members' bills wasn't the path to success; the government must legislate. Two months later, Keir Hardie led an effort to pass a bill to help the unemployed in an economy in which unemployment was increasing. Prime Minister Arthur Balfour's government attempted to postpone the bill. Several thousand destitute workers marched from the East End to Westminster in protest. In Manchester, mobs of enraged unemployed men marched in the streets, and four men were arrested. Ten days later, Arthur Balfour backed down, and the bill became law.

This success was not lost on the women of the WSPU. They had noticed that the threat of violence had caused the government to act. If a threat of violence was required to get bills passed into law, then they would become increasingly militant. Sylvia observed, "It was only a question of how militant tactics would begin." The Pankhursts initiated a nationwide militant movement operating out of Manchester and led by Christabel.

Esther Roper, Women's Rights leader who was impressed with Christabel's skill in arguing issues, suggested to Emmeline that her oldest daughter should study law. Emmeline asked Lord Haldane to sponsor Christabel as a student at Lincoln's Inn, where her father had studied. Lord Haldane agreed, but her application was rejected because women weren't allowed to practice at the Bar. She enrolled at Manchester University's law school instead, while continuing to participate in suffrage work.

In June 1906, Christabel graduated with honors and used her new skills to support the women's cause. She focused on one overriding goal—obtaining the vote for women. All other causes, including social reform issues, were going to have to wait.

Christabel's first unladylike step occurred in 1904 at the Liberal Party meeting at the Free Trade Hall in Manchester at which Winston Churchill launched the campaign for the general election. When a resolution supporting free trade was agreed upon and the speeches were over, Christabel rose from her chair on the platform and asked the chairman if she could propose an amendment on women's suffrage. The chairman denied her request amid cries from the audience, and Christabel backed down.

Later, she recalled, "This was the first militant step—the hardest for me because it was the first. To move from my place on the platform to the speaker's table in the teeth of the astonishment and opposition of will of that immense throng, those civic and county leaders and those Members of Parliament, was the most difficult thing I have ever done." However, it was "a protest of which little was heard and nothing remembered—because it did not result in imprisonment!" She formed the opinion that she must go to prison to arouse public opinion; she must become a martyr.

In 1905, Christabel and her friend, Annie Kenney, attended a Liberal Party rally in the Free Trade Hall in Manchester. Christabel had told her mother, "We shall sleep in prison tonight." They carried a banner that asked: "Will you [the Liberal Party] give votes for women?" Both Annie and Christabel asked the question on their banner. The Chief Constable of Manchester told them that their question would be answered later. It was ignored, so they asked it again. The crowd responded, "Throw them out!"

Stewards bruised and scratched them while attempting to remove them from the hall. Christabel realized that they hadn't done enough to be taken to prison. She knew that she was going to have to do more to be arrested; however, she wasn't sure how to do that with her arms held behind her back. Finally, she was arrested and charged with "spitting at a policeman."

Christabel's account of the incident was, "It was not a real spit, but only, shall we call it, a 'pout,' a perfectly dry purse of the mouth. I could not really have done it, even to get the vote, I think." She was kept in jail for seven days; Annie was jailed for three days. Christabel received the publicity that she sought. Unfortunately, it was not clear that it helped the suffrage cause.

Sylvia and Annie interrupted a speech in Sheffield by Herbert Asquith, Chancellor of the Exchequer, and were jostled by the stewards. Men in the crowd hit them with fists and umbrellas as the women were roughly forced from the hall.

The Pankhursts decided to spread their activities to London. Unfortunately, they didn't have the finances to do it. They were eternal optimists; they thought, "That, too, will come." Annie Kenney was sent to London to spread their version of militant suffrage activity with £2 in her pocketbook. Emmeline Pankhurst instructed her: "Go and rouse London."

The necessary financing did come to them. Frederick and Emmeline ("the other Emmeline") Pethick-Lawrence were visiting South Africa when they heard of the suffragist activities in England. They hurried home to see what they could do to help. The Pethick-Lawrences were philanthropists who had contributed to university settlements and women's hospitals and had founded boys' clubs. They expanded the scope of their monthly newspaper, the *Labour Record*, from supporting the Labour cause to also supporting the suffragist movement.

Initially, Emmeline Pethick-Lawrence hesitated before backing the Pankhursts. In her autobiography, she observed, "I had no fancy to be drawn into a small group of brave and reckless and quite helpless people who were prepared to dash themselves against the oldest tradition of human civilization as well as one of the strongest governments of modern times." She was moved by Annie Kenney's willingness to "rouse London" with £2 in her pocketbook. "I was amused by Annie's ignorance of what the talk of rousing London would involve and yet thrilled by her courage."

The "other Emmeline" attended a suffragist meeting at Sylvia's lodgings and was impressed with the audacity of the six women who were there. She said, "I found there was no office, no organization, no money—no postage stamps even. It was not without dismay that it was borne on me that somebody had to come to the help of this brave little group and that the finger of fate pointed to me." Emmeline helped to establish the Central Committee of the WSPU and became its honorary treasurer.

Not only was Emmeline Pethick-Lawrence a effective treasurer, she was also a source of many good ideas. Money began to flow in to the movement, including generous contributions from Pethick-Lawrence's husband. Collections were taken at WSPU gatherings, and Keir Hardie raised £300 from supporters of the Independent Labour Party. The Pethick-Lawrences allowed the Pankhursts to use their house at Clements Inn as their base of operations, retaining only the upstairs apartment for their own use in addition to one room as an office for the *Labour Record*. They treated Christabel as a favored daughter.

The *Daily Mail* called the militant suffragists "suffragettes," a name that Christabel liked. In her opinion, the suffragists merely desired the vote, but, if you pronounce the hard g, the suffragettes "mean to get it." Membership in the WSPU grew rapidly. Middle class women joined because they were looking for "wider and more important activities and interests." Women of the upper class were drawn to the WSPU for other reasons.

Sylvia noted that "daughters of rich families were often without personal means, or permitted a meager dress allowance, and when their parents died, they were often reduced to genteel penury, or unwelcome dependence on relatives." Sylvia decided that with workers of the lower class, the middle class, and the upper class all joining the suffragettes, she was going to have to be a more active participant herself and spend less time on her artistic pursuits.

Sylvia and Christabel began to have different views on the

movement. Sylvia advocated social reform along with women's suffrage; Christabel focused on the suffragettes' activity. Christabel began to move away from the Labour Party, including Keir Hardie. Sylvia didn't think they should separate themselves from Labour Party support, particularly when Keir Hardie was elected chairman of the group of twenty-nine Labour MPs.

The command of the movement became a triumvirate: Christabel and the two Emmelines. There was no question as to who was in charge; it was Christabel. Some women were surprised how willingly Emmeline Pankhurst followed the direction of her oldest daughter.

In early 1906, thirty women carrying banners marched in front of the residence of the Chancellor of the Exchequer, Herbert Asquith. The marchers were punched and kicked by police, who attempted to break up the march. Annie Kenney and two other suffragettes were sent to jail for six weeks, and Emmeline Pankhurst was handled roughly for asking a question at one of Asquith's meetings. In October 1906, ten women were arrested for making speeches in the lobby of Parliament.

Sylvia went to their aid at the Cannon Row Police Court and was thrown into the street and arrested for obstruction and abusive language. She spent fourteen days in the Third Division of Holloway Prison. In the Third Division, the lowest division, the women were considered common criminals. They ate prison food, were subjected to coarse treatment, and wore prison clothing. Treatment in the Second Division was marginally better. Prisoners in the First Division enjoyed many privileges, including the right to have friends visit, to wear their own clothing, and to have food, writing materials, and other amenities from the outside world.

In 1907, the triumvirate called a Women's Parliament near Westminster to coincide with the opening of Parliament. When they heard that there had been no mention of women's suffrage in the King's Speech, 400 women stormed Parliament. Sylvia described the activities of the constables:

> Mounted men scattered the marchers; foot police
> seized them by the back of the neck and rushed
> them along at arm's length, thumping them in the
> back, and bumping them with their knees in

approved police fashion. Women, by the hundred, returned again and again with painful persistence, enduring this treatment by the hour. Those who took refuge in doorways were dragged down by the steps and hurled in front of the horses, then pounced on by the constables and beaten again.

Fifty women were arrested, including Christabel and Sylvia. Sentences ranged from one to three weeks. This time, the women were placed in the First Division.

Emmeline Pankhurst was asked by the Registrar-General of the Guardians to give up her suffrage activities. She resigned her position as registrar, giving up her job and the income and pension that accompanied it. She said that she was willing to give up her life, if necessary.

In 1908 at the by-election in mid-Devon, Emmeline Pankhurst and a fellow suffragist were attacked by a gang of young Liberal toughs, who were unhappy that their candidate had lost to the Tory candidate. Mrs. Pankhurst was knocked unconscious into the mud and injured her ankle. The young toughs were about to stuff her into a barrel and roll her down main street, when she was rescued by mounted police. The effects of the ankle injury persisted for months and motivated her to work harder for the vote.

Christabel decided that the next step was for her mother to go to jail. From a small cart, the injured Emmeline led a delegation of thirteen women who marched on Parliament. All thirteen women were sent to prison for six months in the Second Division. In her first visit to prison Emmeline tolerated the stripping, the body search, the bath in filthy water, and the patched and stained prison clothing made of coarse material.

Emmeline knew that the cold cells and the plank bed would be uncomfortable, but she was unprepared for the sobbing and foul language of the other prisoners. In particular, she was affected by the claustrophobic living conditions of many women in a small cell. Within two days, dyspepsia, migraine headaches, and neuralgia caused her to be moved to the prison hospital.

Another march on Parliament was planned. The Pankhursts weren't sure which verb to use. They considered "besiege," "invade," "raid," and "storm," and finally settled on "rush," which was enough of an action word to provoke the government. They circulated a leaflet with the message, "Men and Women—Help the Suffragettes to Rush the House of Commons," and Christabel and Emmeline spoke in Trafalgar Square. Their call to action was heard by Lloyd George, Chancellor of the Exchequer, and they were charged with "inciting the public to a certain wrongful and illegal act—to rush the House of Commons."

Christabel conducted her own defense and that of the other two women in their trial at Bow Street. The magistrate rejected her request for a trial by jury, but she managed to call Lloyd George and Herbert Gladstone, the Home Secretary, as witnesses. The public was captivated by a young woman lawyer cross-examining cabinet ministers. The suffrage movement received much publicity, but, after two days, Emmeline was sentenced to three months in the Second Division and Christabel to ten weeks. During the trial, Max Beerbohm was impressed with Christabel. He noted in the *Saturday Review* "the contrast between the buoyancy of the girl and the depression of the statesman [Lloyd George]."

While her mother and her sister were in jail, Sylvia planned a rally at Albert Hall, where Lloyd George was to speak. She stayed at suffrage headquarters and waited for women to return from the speech. They were bruised and their clothing was in disarray. Some had their corsets ripped off and their false teeth knocked out. One woman had been whipped with a dog whip, and another had a wrist burned by a man using it to put out his cigar while other men struck her in the chest. The Manchester *Guardian* reported that the women had been treated "with a brutality that was almost nauseating."

The more activist members of the movement became impatient with the government's delays. They threw stones wrapped in WSPU literature through the windows of government buildings. When they were arrested, they went on hunger strikes. Women who were prevented from attending public meetings climbed onto the roof of the hall and used axes to chop off slates. One woman was imprisoned for throwing an iron bar through the window of an empty railroad car on the train carrying the Prime Minister back to London.

The women were given sentences ranging from two weeks to four months. Many of them went on hunger strikes. The Home Secretary ordered that they be forcibly fed using rubber tubes through their mouth or nose. In one case, the feeding tube was accidentally passed into the trachea instead of the esophagus, and the woman developed pneumonia from broth forced into her lung.

Sylvia described being forcibly fed in graphic terms. She experienced shivering and heart palpitations when told that she was going to be forcibly fed. Six big, strong wardresses pushed her down on her back in bed and held her by her ankles, knees, hips, elbows, and shoulders.

A doctor entered her room and attempted unsuccessfully to open her mouth. He then tried to push a steel gag through a gap between her teeth, making her gums bleed. Next two doctors thrust a pointed steel instrument between her jaws, which were forced open by the turn of a screw, and forced a tube down her throat. While Sylvia panted and heaved, she tried to move her head away. She was almost unconscious when they poured the broth into her throat. As soon as the tube was withdrawn, she vomited. She said: "They left me on the bed exhausted, gasping for breath, and sobbing convulsively." The women received this treatment twice a day.

Women began to die for their beliefs in the women's cause. In December 1910, Celia Haig, a sturdy, healthy woman, died of a painful illness caused by injuries incurred when she was assaulted at a public gathering. Mary Clarke, Emmeline Pankhurst's sister, died of a stroke after being released from prison "too frail to weather this rude tide of militant struggle." Henria Williams, who had a weak heart, died in January 1911 from injuries suffered during a rally.

Early in 1912, Emmeline Pankhurst broke several windows at the Prime Minister's residence at 10 Downing Street. She went to jail for two months with 218 other women. In March 1912, the police raided WSPU headquarters and arrested Emmeline and Frederick Pethick-Lawrence. Christabel had recently moved into an apartment and wasn't at Clements Inn when the police arrived. It was obvious to Christabel that the "ringleaders" were being rounded up. She fled to France to ensure the movement's leaders weren't all in jail. Annie Kenney was her link with Clements Inn.

Frederick and the two Emmelines were sent to prison for seven months in the Second Division. Emmeline Pankhurst refused to be treated as she had been on her first trip to prison. Sylvia described the scene: "Mrs. Pankhurst, ill from fasting and suspense, grasped the earthen toilet ewer and threatened to fling it at the doctors and wardresses, who appeared with the feeding tube. They withdrew and the order for her release was issued the next day." Emmeline Pethick-Lawrence was forcibly fed once, and her husband for five days; they, too, were released early.

The movement's militant wing began to set fire to buildings. Sylvia suspected that Christabel was behind this phase of their effort. They burned down churches, historic places, and empty buildings. They tried to set fire to Nuneham House, the home of Lewis Harcourt, an anti-suffragist minister. Two women attempted to burn down the Royal Theatre in Dublin, where Herbert Asquith was scheduled to speak. Christabel's mother convinced her that increased militancy was the direction in which to move. This caused a rift with the Pethick-Lawrences, who preferred a more moderate approach. When they returned from a trip to Canada, the couple who had contributed so much effort and money to the campaign found that they had been frozen out of the leadership.

Frederick Pethick-Lawrence commented on their falling out in unselfish terms. "Thus ended our personal association with two of the most remarkable women I have ever known. They cannot be judged by ordinary standards of conduct; and those who run up against them must not complain of the treatment they receive."

Emmeline Pethick-Lawrence didn't accept the split with the Pankhursts as easily as her husband did. She observed, "There was something quite ruthless about Mrs. Pankhurst and Christabel where human relationships were concerned." The couple recognized Christabel's intelligence and political acumen as well as her appeal to young men and young women. They also appreciated Mrs. Pankhurst's ability to move an audience with her appeals to their emotions by modulating her voice.

The level of destruction caused by the suffragettes stepped up as they became increasingly frustrated with the delay in obtaining the vote, including:

- widespread burning with acid of the message "votes for women" on golf greens
- cutting telephone wires
- burning of boathouses and sports pavilions, including the grandstand at Ayr racecourse
- slashing of thirteen paintings at the Manchester Art Gallery

and the Rokeby "Venus" at the National Gallery
- destroying with a bomb a home being built for Lloyd George
- smashing the glass orchid house at Kew Gardens
- breaking a jewel case in the Tower of London
- burning of three Scottish castles and the Carnegie Library in Birmingham
- flooding the organ in Albert Hall
- exploding a bomb in Westminster Abbey

Emmeline Pankhurst was charged with "counseling and procuring" the blowing up of the house being constructed for Lloyd George at Walton-on-the-Hill. That bombing was done by Emily Wilding Davison, one of the most impulsive suffragettes. To protest not being granted the vote, Davison waited at the turn at Tattenham Corner and committed suicide by throwing herself under the King's horse at the Derby.

The militancy of the movement in England ceased with the outbreak of World War I. Christabel moved back to England, confident that the government would have more on its mind than pursuing her. She announced, "This was national militancy. As suffragettes we could not be pacifists at any price. We offered our service to the country and called upon all our members to do likewise." Christabel supported Asquith in the war effort as fervently as she had opposed him prior to the war. In August 1916, Asquith surprised the House of Commons by declaring that if the voting franchise were expanded, women had an "unanswerable" case for being offered the vote. He observed that "during this war the women of this country have rendered as effective a service in the prosecution of the war as any other class of the community."

In February 1917, a committee recommended that the vote be granted to all men over twenty-one and women over thirty who were university graduates or local government electors (owners or tenant householders), or the wives of both. The bill was extended to the wives of all voters and became law in January 1918. Eight and a half million women were enfranchised. Ten years later, the remaining political limitations on women were removed.

Emmeline Pankhurst died in June 1928, a month before her seventieth birthday. Christabel wrote, "The House of Lords passed the final measure of Votes for Women in the hour her body, which had suffered so much for that cause, was laid in the grave. She, who had come to them in their need, had stayed with the women as long as they might still need her, and then she went away."

In 1936, Christabel was made a Dame Commander of the British Empire for "public and social services." She moved to the United States and died in Santa Monica, California, in 1958.

The Pankhursts were a family of achievers. Perhaps the characteristic that led to their many accomplishments was best summarized by Frederick and Emmeline Pethick-Lawrence: "Their absolute refusal to be deflected by criticism or deviate one hair's breadth from the course they had determined to pursue. Men and women of destiny are like that."

MARGARET SANGER—Birth Control Reformer

"Sanger's goal was to bring safe and legal methods of birth control to the women of America. Within her lifetime, this goal was achieved—almost miraculously, since she was born in a era when the concept of birth control was not discussed or supported publically, when there still was no formal education available on how pregnancy comes about, and when any printed information on sex was considered a violation of federal law."

Elyse Topalian, *Margaret Sanger*

Margaret Higgins Sanger had first-hand experience of the impact of large families on the health and well-being of the mother. Her own mother, Anne Higgins, whose health was never robust, died of tuberculosis at the age of forty-eight while laboring with the burden of raising eleven children. Anne Higgins's struggle was complicated by the fact that the family was poor.

While completing her nurses' training at the Manhattan Eye and Ear Institute, Margaret met William Sanger, an architect who had a contract with the institute. Sanger was captivated by Margaret, and he pursued her until she accepted his proposal. They were married on August 18, 1902.

Sanger's experience in making public speeches began in New York with a request from the editor of the socialist newspaper, the *Call*, to fill in for a speaker who had cancelled on short notice. She spoke about the economic problems of the working-class poor and the general problems of family life.

These speaking engagements led to a request from the *Call* to write a series of articles on motherhood issues in which Sanger addressed the functions of the reproductive organs, the physiology of a woman's body, and venereal disease. The twelve-part series was called "What Every Woman Should Know." Although articles on these subjects are common today, they were not in 1913.

The main obstacle to publishing such articles was the Comstock Law of 1873, named for Anthony Comstock, an official of the U.S. Post Office. Comstock had the authority to open mail and rule whether the contents of the mail were within his guidelines of decency, that is, whether or not in his judgement they were obscene. Comstock was ultraconservative, and Sanger's series of articles on the subject of venereal disease didn't fall within his guidelines of decency. He notified the *Call* that if they published Sanger's next article on venereal disease, he would revoke their mailing permit. The following week, the women's page of the *Call* was blank except for the words: "What Every Girl Should Know— Nothing! By Order of the Post Office Department."

After taking time off, Sanger returned to work as a nurse, partly for economic reasons and partly because she needed to be active. Most women gave birth in the home, and nurses attended to the new mother until she was back on her feet. Many calls for Sanger's care were from the Lower East Side, where many of Manhattan's poor lived. Frequently, she was asked the same question that she received as a student nurse: "Tell me how to avoid having another baby for a while. We cannot afford another one yet."

The only information that Sanger could give involved preventative measures that the husband could take. The women didn't want that information; they wanted to know what steps they could take personally to prevent conception. The women didn't believe that Sanger had nothing to tell them. They thought that if they had enough money to buy the information she would sell it to them, and that rich people knew birth prevention techniques that the poor didn't. It did not console them when Sanger told them that wealthy people knew no more about the subject than they did.

Sanger was frustrated with her inability to provide these struggling women with useful information. She wanted to address the root cause of the problem, uncontrolled procreation, but realized that nursing wasn't the arena to address the problem most efficiently. Sanger tried to find as much information as she could on the subject of contraception. She spent the next six months doing research and was surprised how little information existed on the subject. One of the few references she could find was a book written over fifty years previously by a Massachusetts physician.

Sanger went to Europe to look for additional reference material on contraception. She visited France, which had one of the lowest birthrates in Europe. French women investigated means of contraception and then passed the information on from one generation to the next. When Margaret had enough material to pass on to women in the United States, she went home.

Upon her return to New York, Sanger edited and published a magazine called *The Woman Rebel*. Comstock reacted promptly. He reviewed his complaints with the Postmaster General, and Sanger received a letter stating: "In accordance with advice from the Assistant Attorney General for the Post Office Department, you are informed that the publication entitled *The Woman Rebel* for March 1914 is unmailable."

The Post Office confiscated half of the shipment of the March issue. Sanger and her helpers worked overtime addressing new copies to replace the ones that the Post Office Department had confiscated. The April and June issues were circulated with no problems, but the Post Office prevented the May, July, and August issues from being mailed.

Concurrently with her work on *The Woman Rebel*, Sanger wrote *Family Limitation*, a pamphlet in which she described contraceptive techniques. She wrote it in a very straightforward style and supplemented the text with diagrams. She described the birth control devices available to women and how to use them.

She had difficulty in finding a printer; in fact, twenty-two printers turned her down. One said, "That can never be printed. That's a Sing Sing job." Finally, she found a printer who would print her pamphlet. He printed 100,000 in off hours, so that his employees wouldn't know about it.

In August, Sanger was notified that she had been indicted by the United States government on nine counts of violation of the criminal code, and, if convicted on all counts, the maximum sentence was forty-five years in jail. She received no notice of when she was due in court. Several weeks later, she received a call asking why she hadn't appeared in court that morning. She requested a postponement and was told that her case was proceeding that afternoon.

She consulted a lawyer who asked the court for a postponement; he was given until the following morning. Since they didn't have time to prepare a case, Sanger's attorney advised her to plead guilty so he could negotiate with the district attorney for a fine and avoid a jail term. She decided not to plead guilty; she didn't think she had received fair treatment in her request for a postponement to prepare the case. She decided to run and to fight another time. She went to Canada and then sailed for England using an assumed name.

In England, Sanger met Havelock Ellis, an essayist, psychologist, and author of the seven-volume work, *The Psychology of Sex.* Although Ellis had received medical training and specialized in obstetrics, he was known as a sexual reformer. Havelock Ellis had a great influence on Sanger's thinking; she considered it a privilege to know him. They became friends, and he was a frequent advisor.

Sanger went to Holland, where the birthrate was dropping, but the death rate was declining even faster, causing a net gain in population. Their birthrate was dropping because the Dutch had liberal views about birth control. In 1878, Dr. Aletta Jacobs, the first woman medical doctor in Holland, had established the first birth control clinic in the world. Between 1878 and 1915, birth control clinics were established around Holland.

The leadership of the National Birth Control League that Sanger had founded before she left for Europe had passed to others. She attended a meeting of their executive committee upon her return from Europe to inquire about the support she could expect from the league during her trial. They responded that she could expect no support; they were an organization that obeyed the law. The goal of the league was to work to get the laws changed, and they wouldn't support a person who had broken the law.

The general public was more supportive of Sanger than her friends and advisors were. They advised her to compromise to avoid going to jail. An arrangement was made with the District Attorney for Sanger to promise she wouldn't break the law again in return for dropping her case. She wasn't receptive to this, because she didn't feel that she had broken the obscenity law. She rejected legal support and conducted her own defense at her trial.

Both the District Attorney and the judge received many communications in support of Sanger. Nine distinguished Englishmen, including Arnold Bennett and H. G. Wells, sent a letter to President Wilson requesting him to intervene in her defense. The level of support for Sanger motivated the judge to postpone the case three times. Finally, on February 18, her case was dismissed. She felt that she had been vindicated; however, legally, nothing had been settled. Her cause received national exposure, and she was now free to continue her efforts.

On October 16, 1916, Sanger opened her first birth control clinic in Brooklyn. She publicized the opening of the clinic, and 140 women visited it the first day. On the tenth day of its operation, the police impounded her equipment, files, and birth control literature, and interviewed clients to obtain information to be used against Sanger in court. She received a sentence of thirty days in the workhouse and gave birth control lectures while there. The matron objected, but Sanger persisted. Upon her release from prison, Sanger made a movie, *The Hand That Rocks the Cradle,* to spread the word about birth control. It wasn't permitted to be shown in public because it contained the words "birth control."

Sanger began to publish a magazine called the *Birth Control Review*. Havelock Ellis and H. G. Wells contributed articles on economic and social topics that were population-related. At first, the magazine struggled financially, but it received wide support by influential women and prospered. It was the principal publication of the birth control movement for twenty-three years.

Sanger's lawyer appealed her conviction for operating the Brooklyn clinic. Her appeal to the Appellate Division was defeated, but her appeal to the Court of Appeals of New York State was upheld by Judge Frederick Crane on January 18, 1918. The decision became known as the Crane decision.

Sanger considered the impact of this decision to be monumental. Clinics could be established in which physicians could inform women about birth control techniques. In her opinion, the birth control movement had been placed where it should be; the medical profession could oversee it. In 1921, recognizing a need for an organization to provide direction and to solicit financial support, Sanger formed the American Birth Control League. The League is still in existence as Planned Parenthood of America. In 1929, Sanger established the Birth Control Clinical Research Bureau. The Birth Control League referred patients to the bureau. In April 1929, the bureau was raided by the police; they had a general warrant, and they impounded the bureau's records. Public opinion was strongly against this violation of the doctor / patient relationship.

Sanger's last battle was the support of a federal "Doctors' Bill" to overturn the Comstock Law, which was still in effect forbidding the use of the U.S. mail to import or distribute contraceptive devices and information. Her goal was to change the penal code to allow this material to be shipped via mail. Congress couldn't obtain a majority to pass a bill to change the law, however.

In 1933, a package containing birth control devices addressed to the director of the Birth Control Research Bureau was seized by the Post Office. The director filed charges to force the case to go to court. On January 6, 1936, the judge ruled that the director should receive her package. The government appealed but lost the appeal. The appeals judge stated that the Comstock Law's "design, in our opinion, was not to prevent the importation, sale or carriage by mail of things which might intelligently be employed by conscientious and competent physicians for the purpose of saving life or promoting the well-being of their patients."

The government decided not to take its case to the Supreme Court. Sanger wrote in the *Birth Control News* that the decision "brings to an end the sixty-three year reign of muddle and tyranny inaugurated by the so-called Comstock legislation enacted in 1873 and clarifies once and for all future time the position and rights of the American physician in the legitimate use of scientific contraceptives." Support for the birth control movement continued, and on June 10, 1937, the American Medical Association resolved that doctors should be informed of their rights in prescribing contraceptives and in educating the public on the subject. Two of Margaret Sanger's observations typify her outlook on life:

> Some lives drift here and there like reeds in a stream, depending on changing currents for their activity. Others are like swimmers knowing the depth of the water. Each stroke helps them onward to a definite objective.

> Life has taught me one supreme lesson: this is that we must—if we are really to live at all—put our convictions into action.

* * *

Emmeline Pankhurst and her family were certainly assertive and aggressive in leading the Women's Rights Movement in England, as was Margaret Sanger in leading the unpopular birth control movement in the U.S. If we asserted ourselves about our convictions a fraction of what these women did, we could be more successful.

CHAPTER 10

RELATIONSHIPS—ROLE MODELS

Elizabeth Barrett Browning (1806-1861) Poet

Frederick Delius (1862-1934) Composer

"The art of relationships is, in large part, skill in managing emotions in others. Social competence and incompetence, and the specific skills involved are the abilities that undergrid popularity, leadership, and interpersonal effectiveness. People who do well in these skills do well at anything that relies on interacting smoothly with others; they are the social stars. Talent, that of empathy and connecting makes it easy to enter into an encounter or to recognize and respond fittingly to people's feelings and concerns—the art of relationship."

Daniel Goleman, *Emotional Intelligence:*
Why It Can Matter More Than IQ

ELIZABETH BARRETT BROWNING—Poet

"How do I love thee? Let me count the ways.
I love thee to the depth and breadth and height
My soul can reach, when feeling out of sight
For the ends of Being and ideal Grace.
I love thee to the level of every day's
Most quiet need, by sun and candlelight.
I love thee freely, as men strive for Right;
I love thee purely, as men turn from Praise.
I love thee with the passion put to use
In my old griefs, and with my childhood's faith.
I love thee with a love I seemed to lose
With my lost saints,—I love thee with the breath,
Smiles, tears, of all my life!—and, if God choose,
I shall love thee better after death."

Elizabeth Barrett Browning, *Sonnets from the Portuguese*

Elizabeth Barrett's reputation as a poet exceeded that of Robert Browning when they met. She was an invalid who rarely left her room in her parents' home. Initially, they corresponded, and Robert arranged their meeting through a mutual friend. Each had a strong respect for the other's poetry, and they found that they had much in common emotionally. Elizabeth's father had forbidden his children, both sons and daughters, to marry. Since Elizabeth was chronically ill, she wasn't concerned about this parental edict until she met Robert. Her health improved as their love for each other developed.

Elizabeth and Robert were married secretly, eloped, and moved to Italy. Elizabeth was disowned by her father, but she had a small annuity on which to live. Robert's income was not sufficient to support them. They remained deeply in love and had an idyllic marriage. They had no serious arguments, and each was strongly supportive of the other's writing. In her opinion, she had not begun to live until she met Robert. Ultimately, with her advice and editing, Robert's poetry gained a wider acceptance than his earlier works, and her poetry was also improved by his advice and suggestions. Elizabeth's story cannot be told without also telling the story of Robert.

Elizabeth Barrett, the oldest child of Edward Moulton Barrett and Mary Graham-Clarke Barrett, was born on March 6, 1806, in Durham, England. Edward Barrett was a wealthy merchant whose family owned a plantation in Jamaica. Elizabeth received no formal education, but she read widely and, to a large extent, was self-educated. She learned Greek by participating in her brother Edward's lessons. Her first poems, including "The Battle of Marathon," were published when she was thirteen. Her father paid for a private printing of her early poems.

In 1832, the Barrett family moved to Devon and three years later moved to London. In 1838, they moved to 50 Wimpole Street, which was popularized in Rudolf Besier's play, *The Barretts of Wimpole Street*. She published *The Serafim and Other Poems* that year and suffered a serious health problem that affected her respiratory system, which possibly involved abscesses in the lungs. Her health deteriorated to the point that she was considered an invalid.

By1841, Elizabeth was a complete invalid. She spent her days reclining on a sofa and rarely left her room. She received few visitors and did not envision much of a future for herself. However, she wrote many letters and stayed current in the literary world by corresponding with scholars and writers of the day.

In 1844, Elizabeth's reputation as a poet was enhanced by the publication of her new book of poems, which included "A Drama of Exile" (about the exile of Adam and Eve from Paradise), twenty-eight sonnets, some romantic ballads, and miscellaneous other poems. These poems elevated her standing with the critics and brought her to the attention of a fellow poet, Robert Browning.

Robert Browning, oldest child of Robert Browning, Sr., and Sarah Weidemann Browning, was born at Camberwell, England, on May 7, 1812. Robert Browning, Sr., was a bibliophile and scholar who worked for the Bank of England for fifty years. Young Robert grew up in a home with thousands of books. He attended private schools in his neighborhood, but most of his education was received at home with his father serving as one of his tutors. His education was almost exclusively literary and musical. He lived at home until he married at the age of thirty-three.

In his twenties, Robert was a prolific author, writing "Paracelsus," "Sordello," "Bells and Pomegranates," "Pippa Passes," and five plays: *King Victor and King Charles, The Return of the Druses, Columbe's Birthday, Strafford,* and *A Blot in the 'Scutcheon.* The last two had very short runs on the stage, and the other dramas were not produced. He was not considered a successful playwright.

Robert had a full social life, and he had many literary friends including John Forster, literary critic of *The Examiner.* Initially, Forster was the only critic to perceive the merit of "Paracelsus." Thomas Carlyle became a lifelong friend. Robert had many women friends but had no close attachments with women. That was about to change.

Elizabeth was ambitious and wanted to break out of the shell that her illness had imposed on her. She did not think of love and sexual passion, but she wanted to find another person with whom she could share poetic passion. When she read "Paracelsus," she suspected that Robert Browning might be that poet. Most of what she knew of Robert was from his poetry and her interpretation of it. She knew a few things about Robert, the man, from her distant cousin, John Kenyon.

In late December 1844, Robert returned from a trip to Italy and read Elizabeth Barrett's collection of poems that had been published the preceding August. He admired her poetry and heard more about her from his friend and her cousin, John Kenyon. Robert wrote to Elizabeth to tell her how much he enjoyed her poetry.

In his first letter to her, Robert said, "I love your verses with all my heart, dear Miss Barrett." He did not attempt to analyze her poetry; he said that "into me it has gone, and part of me it has become, this great living poetry of yours, not a flower of which but took root and grew. I do, as I say, love these books with all my heart—and I love you too."

Elizabeth replied that she was delighted with "the sympathy of a poet, and such a poet!" She asked him for criticisms of her writing and offered some comments on his efforts: "'Misty' is an infamous word for your kind of obscurity. You are never misty—not even in 'Sordello'—never vague. Your graver cuts deep sharp lines, always—and there is an extra-distinctness in your images and thoughts, from the midst of which, crossing each other infinitely, the general significance seems to escape."

They corresponded frequently. Over 600 of their letters survived, providing a wealth of personal information for biographers.

In one of her letters to him, she offered her views on writing: "Like to write? Of course, of course I do. I seem to live while I write—it is life, for me. Why, what is to live? Not to eat and drink and breathe—but to feel the life in you down all the fibers of being, passionately and joyfully. And thus, one lives in composition surely—not always—but when the wheel goes round and the process is uninterrupted."

Initially, their letters were about their craft, but soon the relationship deepened. On May 20, 1845, they met for the first time. After that meeting, Robert wrote to her, concluding his letter: "I am proud and happy in your friendship—now and forever. May God bless you!" He followed that letter with one declaring his love. He was moving too fast for her. She responded, "You do not know what pain you give me by speaking so wildly. You have said some intemperate things, fancies, which you will not say over again, nor unsay, but forget at once." He replied that she had misunderstood him; she accepted his explanation.

Robert's letters give the impression of a man attempting to control an overwhelming emotion. Her letters in response provide a recurring theme; she is unworthy, and she fears that she will encumber him because her poor health will limit his social activity. Elizabeth's other problem in addition to her health concerns was her autocratic father's refusal to allow any of his children to marry.

Elizabeth held him off, viewing him as the giver and herself as the taker; she felt that she was not good enough for him. Ultimately, they acknowledged to each other that they were very much in love, and they began to plan their marriage. Two months before their wedding, she told him that he would be better off if he left her.

Elizabeth and Robert planned to be married in secret and then wait for a time when her father was away to leave for a honeymoon in Italy. Elizabeth told her sisters of her plans, but would not allow them to attend the wedding ceremony because it would upset their father. She did not tell her brothers or most of her close friends about her wedding plans. They were married in St. Marylebone parish church on September 12, 1846.

On September 19, accompanied by her maid, the Brownings left for Italy. Elizabeth had almost fifteen years of happy married life and creative professional life ahead of her. She gave birth to a son in 1849, and in 1861, after a flurry of loving kisses, died peacefully in Robert's arms.

Their letters provide a comprehensive look at the complexity of their relationship. They even corresponded when Robert was away on a short trip to find a place to stay for the summer away from the heat of Florence. Both correspondents were able to express their feelings superbly in writing.

While living at the Casa Guidi in Florence after the birth of their son, Weidemann ("Pen"), Elizabeth showed Robert the poems that she had written during their courtship but had never let him read. She had traced their courtship from hesitation, doubt, and reservation to the happiness of reciprocated love. They were personal poems, and she suspected he would not like them published.

To the contrary, Robert considered them among the best sonnets in the English language. "When Robert saw them he was much touched and pleased—and thinking highly of the poetry he could not consent, he said, that they should be lost to my volumes [of 1850] and so we agreed to slip them in under some sort of veil, and after much consideration chose the 'Portuguese.'" The collection of forty-three sonnets was entitled *Sonnets from the Portuguese.*

Robert completed two volumes of poetry entitled *Men and Women* while living in Florence. Elizabeth worked on *Aurora Leigh*, a novel in verse that she described as "the novel or romance I have been hankering after for so long." She described it to her brother, George, as "beyond question my best work."

In Elizabeth's verse novel, Aurora Leigh is born in Italy to an English father and an Italian mother, from whom she is orphaned at the age of thirteen. A disciplinarian aunt in England, who raised her, wants her to marry her cousin, but Aurora wants to become a poet. Elizabeth addresses the question in her work of whether women can be happy with just their art or if they need men to feel fulfilled. Her cousin proposes to a poor girl who jilts him. Elizabeth uses an intricate plot to tell her "thoroughly modern" story.

Elizabeth told her sister Arabel, "Robert and I work every day—he has a large volume of short poems which will be completed by the spring—and I have some four thousand, five hundred lines of mine—I am afraid six thousand lines will not finish it." To protect their work schedule, they did not receive visitors before three o'clock. Elizabeth wrote in the drawing room, and Robert worked in the sitting room. The doors to the dining room in between these two rooms remained closed. She wrote in an armchair with her feet raised; he worked at a desk.

Although Elizabeth and Robert edited each other's completed work, they did not review each other's daily effort nor did they discuss their work every day. Elizabeth, in particular, had strong feelings about this. She thought that no matter how close two people are to each other, that closeness should not extend to their work. She said, "An artist must, I fancy, either find or make solitude to work in, if it is to be good work at all." Until her work was completed, she kept the details to herself.

The Brownings visited London to oversee the printing of Robert's *Men and Women*. Elizabeth pitched in and read the proofs as they came off the press. The effort was very exhausting for her, but she was convinced that this work would enhance her husband's reputation. Her effort to complete *Aurora Leigh* was postponed.

Men and Women was successful initially; the first edition sold out immediately, and American publishers requested the rights to reprint it. Elizabeth had helped Robert to be clearer in expressing his artistic feelings. Critics were no longer calling his work obscure. Elizabeth had also helped him to think less of financial concerns and to place more emphasis on writing poems. She considered *Men and Women* a brilliant collection and hoped that his genius would be acclaimed by his peers.

As soon as Elizabeth had completed *Aurora Leigh*, Robert made arrangements to have it published; in effect, he acted as her business manager. Both Elizabeth and Robert read the proofs and prepared the manuscript for the press. He discontinued the promotion of his last collection and postponed work on his next book of poems. Sales of *Men and Women* began to slip; it could have used additional promotion.

Robert took drawing and sculpting lessons in Florence. While they lived in Italy, he was not as dedicated to writing as she was. During their fifteen-year marriage, his poetic output was not as great as hers. Before their marriage, he had lived at home where his sister and his parents had ministered to his needs. He had no responsibilities that diverted him from writing. After he was married, he had to look after Elizabeth, with her delicate health.

Their son, Robert Weidemann Browning ("Pen"), was born on March 9, 1849. Elizabeth wrote poetry while she was pregnant; she completed the first part of "Casa Guidi Windows" during this time. Early in their marriage, Robert learned from Elizabeth; her reputation was greater than his at that stage of their careers. She encouraged him to concentrate on dramatic monologues in poetry and to give up playwriting. She was concerned that he was not measuring up to his potential because of his reduced productivity. He was not concerned; he looked upon it as a temporary condition.

After the birth of their son, Robert began work on a long double poem entitled "Christmas Eve and Easter Day." Elizabeth was a strong influence on the choice of a theme for this work. She suggested that he write from the heart, not the head, and that he convey his own thoughts using a minimum of dramatic devices. She encouraged him to write about his hopes and fears, particularly those of a religious nature, in his poetry.

On January 1, 1852, Elizabeth was pleased to hear that Robert had made a New Year's resolution to write a poem every day. He began with "Love Among the Ruins," "Women and Roses," and "Childe Rolande." However, his writing was not sustained. They were staying in Paris at the time, and he resumed his contacts with society. Elizabeth encouraged this, even though she was unable to accompany him. She experienced social activity vicariously through him and stayed current with the Paris social scene.

Attending social events provided an outlet for Robert at a time when Elizabeth's poor health restricted her mobility. Talk continued to be an important factor in the couple's relationship. They knew that as long as they could be together and communicate freely, Elizabeth's delicate health would not ruin their marriage. This openness extended to instances of minor disagreement.

The Brownings' marriage was solid and enduring. The few disagreements that they had involved viewing some of their friends from different perspectives. Elizabeth could learn from Robert about the nature of people, but she tended to stay with her own evaluation of friends.

Their principal difference of opinion was Elizabeth's belief in spiritualism and in communicating with the dead in seances. They attended sessions with the seer Daniel Douglas Home. Robert remained unconvinced of the value of seances; he wrote a spoof of spiritualism entitled "Mr. Sludge, the Medium."

Elizabeth and Robert retained their own identities. They thought independently and were exciting conversationalists. Neither tried to convert the other to his or her own image of an ideal partner in marriage. Robert wrote to his brother-in-law George, "I shall only say that Ba [Elizabeth] and I know each other for a time and, I dare trust, eternity—We differ as to spirit-rapping, we quarrel sometimes about politics, and estimate people's characters with enormous difference, but, in the main, we know each other, I say."

Elizabeth's health deteriorated during the last three years of her life. When she seemed to be slipping away, the doctor was summoned. She appeared to be sleeping; Robert whispered in her ear, "Do you know me?" She murmured, "My Robert—my heavens, my beloved!" She kissed him repeatedly and said, "Our lives are held by God." He laid her head on the pillow. She tried to kiss him again but could no longer reach him, so she kissed her own hand and extended it to him. Robert asked, "Are you comfortable?" She responded, "Beautiful."

Elizabeth began to fall asleep again, and Robert realized that she should not be in a reclining position when a cough was coming. He raised her up to ease the cough. She began to cough up phlegm but then stopped. Robert was not sure if she had fainted or fallen asleep. He saw her brow contract as though in pain and then relax. She looked very young. Their servant Annunciata, who realized that she was dead, said in Italian, "Her last gesture a kiss, her last thought of love."

Robert's friends expected him to break down completely after the loss of one so close. However, he remained in control, partly because Elizabeth had died so peacefully in his arms. Robert knew that his friends felt sorry for him in his loss. He was extremely grateful for the fifteen years that he and Elizabeth had together. He knew that she had more to give, but he appreciated the rare union that they had. Friends were also concerned about Pen, who had been as close to his mother as a son and a mother can be. He, too, held up well and, in fact, was a consolation to his father.

Elizabeth's place in literary history is summarized by essayist and poet Alice Meynell:

> The place of Elizabeth Barrett Browning in English literature is high, if not on the summits. She had an original genius, a great heart, and an intellect that was, if not great, exceedingly active. She seldom has composure or repose, but it is not true that her poetry is purely emotional. It is full of abundant, and often overabundant thoughts. It is intellectually restless. She "dashed" not by reason of feminine weakness, but as it were to prove her possession of masculine strength. Her gentler work, as in the *Sonnets from the Portuguese*, is beyond praise. There is in her poetic personality a glory of righteousness, of spirituality, and of ardor that makes her name a splendid one in the history of incomparable literature.

Although Elizabeth was only fifty-five when she died, she had achieved the goal she set as a young girl: to produce lasting poetry that made a significant contribution to her era. She influenced other poets, including Emily Dickinson, even before she died.

Elizabeth was not sure that marriage was for her; she knew that the goals of husband, home, and children, by themselves, were not enough. To have found Robert to love and to have her love reciprocated was more than she had hoped for. Having a son at the age of forty-three added to her joy. She never stopped appreciating her good fortune to be poet, wife, and mother. Her remaining goal was for Robert to make the mark in poetry of which she knew he was capable.

Robert and Pen left Florence on July 27, 1861. In September, they arrived in London, where Robert lived for the next twenty-five years. He visited Italy, but he never returned to Florence. Initially, he was lonely, but eventually he resumed his literary connections in society. He published *Dramatis Personae* in 1864, which led to his being lionized. In 1867, Oxford University awarded him a Master of Arts degree and Balliol College elected him an honorary Fellow.

The Ring and the Book, generally regarded as his masterpiece, was published in four volumes in 1868-69. Elizabeth's dreams were at last realized when he was hailed as "a great dramatic poet." In *The Ring and the Book*, which was based on Guido Franceschini's court case in Florence, Browning told the story of a gruesome murder twelve times. He versified the arguments of the counsels for the prosecution and the defense as well as the gossip of busybodies. The story was told with the detail of a court recorder.

In 1881, the Browning Society was formed by Dr. Furnival and Miss E. H. Hickey. Browning received additional honors: a LL.D. degree from Cambridge University in 1879, the D.C.L. from Oxford University in 1882, and a LL.D. degree from Edinburgh University in 1884. In 1886, he became foreign correspondent to the Royal Academy.

During his twenty-eight-year widowhood, privacy was important to him. Robert destroyed all of the letters of his youth and the letters to his family. He could not destroy his wife's letters to him, nor could he destroy his letters to her. However, he was not sure what to do with them. He left them to his son to decide; Pen published them in 1899.

In the Introduction to *How Do I Love Thee?*, V. E. Stack observed: "To read these letters is to be given a marvelously clear vision of great love, and great courage; and to understand something of the complexity of human relationships. That these two poets wrote to each other with so much joy, so much power to express what for most men is inexpressible in language—that is our great good fortune. For Browning and Elizabeth themselves, these written words were a necessity of their love, strongly woven into its very pattern. Browning himself wrote a regretful little epitaph: 'How strange it will be to have no more letters.'"

Robert never ceased promoting Elizabeth's work. He realized that part of his popularity was because he was the widower of Elizabeth Barrett Browning. Robert died on December 12, 1889, while visiting Pen in Venice. His body was brought to London for burial in Westminster Abbey. It was proposed that Elizabeth's body be disinterred from the cemetery in Florence and buried alongside her husband. However, Pen decided that her grave should not be disturbed.

FREDERICK DELIUS—Composer

"I think that the most stupid thing one can do is to spend one's life doing something one hates, or in which he has no interest; in other words, it is a wasted life. I do not believe in sacrificing the big things in life to anyone or anything. Everything depends on your perseverance. One never knows how far one can go. Emerson says in one of his essays, 'A man who works with his whole soul at anything whatever will make it a success before he is fifty,' and I believe this to be perfectly true. One's talent develops like muscles that you are constantly training. Trust more in hard work than inspiration."

Frederick Delius

The music of English composer Frederick Delius is delicate and reserved, perhaps too delicate to be widely appreciated; nevertheless, he is considered one of the masters of music of the early twentieth century. He composed over ninety works, including six operas, four concertos, five pieces of chamber music, and a number of songs. His work is not widely presented.

At its premiére in the fall of 1935, George Gershwin's popular *Porgy and Bess* was hailed as the first Negro opera. Delius's *Koanga*, a Negro opera in three acts with unforgettable melodies, had its premiére at the Stadttheater in Eberfield, Germany, in March 1904. In 1935, it was presented in London by Sir Thomas Beecham at Covent Garden before it was taken on tour.

Delius's choral works include *A Mass of Life*, *Sea Drift*, *A Song of the High Hills*, and *Requiem*. Examples of orchestral works are *Over the Hills and Far Away, Paris: The Song of a Great City, Life's Dance, Brigg Fair* and two exquisite pieces for small orchestra, *Summer Night on the River* and *On Hearing the First Cuckoo in Spring*.

In the Introduction to *Frederick Delius* by Peter Warlock (Philip Heseltine), Hubert Foss compares the man, who continued to compose after going blind and becoming paralyzed, with his music:

> Out of all of this will emerge, I deeply hope, some
> sense of that curiously complicated, yet oddly sim-
> ple character, Frederick Delius. To those who

know the sounds, bathe in the beautiful warm, sun-
lit sea of harmony in his music . . . to those people
it may come as a surprise to discover a character of
immense virility and even obstinacy. "Delius's
music is so tender," said [composer] Norman
O'Neill. The man Delius was not tender but purposeful and projective. The legend that has grown
out of his paralyzed blindness is entirely at vari-
ance with the trapper of dreams himself. The man
Delius was totally unlike his music, the one dis-
playing a most purposeful character, the other a
vivid nebulosity of dreams.

Frederick Delius, the second son of Julius and Elise Krönig
Delius, was born on January 29, 1862, in Bradford, England. Julius
Delius was a successful wool merchant with an international business. He took his children to Manchester to hear the Hallé
Orchestra and to the Theatre Royal in Leeds to attend the opera. He
appreciated music and was a patron of the Hallé Orchestra and willingly paid for music lessons for his children. Young Frederick
chose the violin as his first instrument and also played the piano.
His mother encouraged him to improvise when he played.

Delius was educated at the Bradford Grammar School and the
International School in Isleworth, London. He studied Latin,
Greek, geography, mathematics, natural history, physics, and social
science. He wasn't much of a scholar. Going to school in London
provided him with access to concerts at Covent Garden and St.
James Hall, where he discovered Wagner, Grieg, and Berlioz. Upon
his graduation from the International School, his father expected
him to go into the family business.

Delius went to work for Delius and Company in Bradford but
spent all of his spare hours on music and traveled to London to hear
works by Chopin, Grieg, and Wagner. He was sent to Chemnitz,
Germany, and to Norköpping, Sweden, as a unpaid apprentice to
learn all aspects of the wool industry. While in Sweden, he took
hiking trips to Norway, where he learned Norwegian and was introduced to Ibsen's plays.

Delius was particularly impressed by the lines of Ibsen's clergyman hero in *Brand*:

One thing a man cannot give: his soul.
He cannot deny his calling.
He dare not block that river's course;
It forces its way to the ocean.
A place on earth where one can be wholly oneself:
That is man's right, and I ask no more.

Delius was doing what his father wanted him to do; however, he was not doing it well, and he was certainly not enjoying it.

Julius was disappointed with reports about his son's performance as an unpaid apprentice. Young Frederick had wandered off from the workplace and had attended concerts in Germany and Sweden. Next, Delius was sent to St. Etienne, France, with little money to spend on concerts. He failed there and again as an assistant office manager back home in Bradford. He wanted to attend the Leipzig Music Conservatory, but his father refused to pay his tuition.

Delius saw a poster in Bradford advertising farmland with orange groves in Florida. He told his father that he would like to become an orange grower. His father reluctantly agreed to lease a Florida orange and grapefruit plantation with an option to buy for Delius to manage. Delius and a friend traveled to Solano Grove, which was about forty miles south of Jacksonville. The rundown plantation was cared for by the Anderson family, African-Americans who had worked for the previous owner.

Delius was more fascinated by the Negro music, including hymns and spirituals, than by the challenge of growing oranges and grapefruit. The instruments used were banjos, cowbells, log drums, and seed pods. He was moved by the music, which was about slavery and separation; he entered into, in his words, "a state of illumination" and realized that the only future for him was music. He began to compose music in his head similar to what he had heard at the Anderson home.

On a trip to Jacksonville, Delius met Thomas Ward, organist at the Catholic cathedral in St. Augustine, who gave music lessons in Jacksonville. Ward offered to teach him the basics of harmony and counterpoint and loaned him Hector Berlioz's book on orchestration. Ward moved to Solano Grove to give music lessons to Delius on a rented piano. Delius wanted to capture the Negro music. The only other composer to attempt this was Louis Gottschalk, who had written pieces based on New Orleans music.

When his father found out that Delius was concentrating on music and paying no attention to orange growing, he cut off his allowance. His older brother, Ernest, who had failed at sheep farming in New Zealand, showed up at Solano Grove, and Delius turned over the plantation to him. Delius moved to Jacksonville and gave music lessons. He had many eager students, but he accepted a better opportunity, teaching music at Roanoke Female College in Danville, Virginia.

One of Delius's sponsors at the Roanoke Female College wrote to his father about his success in teaching music and asked him to reconsider sending his son to a music conservatory. Julius Delius gave in and agreed to pay for an eighteen-month course in music theory at the Leipzig Conservatory. Delius received instruction in performing with musical instruments, but he did not receive substantial specific instruction on composing.

Delius composed *Florida*, which was based on the music he had heard there. His professors were not comfortable with his unconventional passages and did not encourage him. However, he had met Edvard Grieg on a hiking trip to Norway; Grieg was very supportive and encouraged him to compose according to his own lights.

Delius moved to Paris to compose while living on a miniscule allowance from his father. He worked on *Magic Fountain*, a opera about the search for the fountain of youth in Florida by a Spaniard named Solano with the help of a Seminole Indian princess, Watawa. It was not successful, but an earlier work, *On the Heights*, about the composer's memories of Norway's mountains, enjoyed a limited success. He worked to improve *Magic Fountain*, as well as *On the Heights*.

In 1896, Delius composed an African-American folk opera, *Koanga*, which was about an African prince captured by slave-traders. The storyline was about planters and overseers on plantations and in the fields, a subject Delius knew from his time in Florida. The instrumentation was for banjos, bones, and fiddles.

While working on *Koanga*, he met a young artist, Helen Sophie Emilie Rosen, who went by her childhood name, Jelka. She loved his music and encouraged him to continue his work on *Koanga*. She fell in love with him, but it took him a long time to realize that he was in love with her.

Jelka painted in the garden of an old rundown house in Grez, a hamlet forty miles south of Paris. Eventually, she bought the house. Delius found it to be a peaceful place in which to compose. His compositions were not selling well. His New York agent told him that his harmonies were too complicated, his melodies were not memorable, and the discords were not appreciated.

Delius finally realized that he was in love with Jelka. He missed her when she left Grez; he realized that he couldn't live without her. They were married on September 23, 1903. He was forty-one; she was thirty-five. Jelka gave up her career in art and devoted the rest of her life to Delius; she did everything that she could, including financial and administrative tasks, to allow her husband to concentrate on composing.

A reporter described Delius at this time:

> He is a pale man, ascetic and monkish; a man with a waspish wit, a man who allows his wit to run away with him so far that he is tempted to express opinions that he does not really hold. He is a man who pursues a path of his own, indifferent to criticism, and perhaps indifferent to indifference. Decidedly a man of most distinguished intellect, and a quick, eager, but not responsive personality. He is about forty years of age, taller than one at first thinks, lean, wiry, strenuous in every movement, a fine face with piercing eyes. Every movement he makes is rapid, decisive; he is a prodigious walker, bicyclist, and swimmer.

A Norwegian playwright, Gunnar Heiberg, wrote a political satire, *The Council of the People*, and asked Delius to write the accompanying music. Since *The Council of the People* was mocking and satirical, Delius wrote the background music, *Norwegian Suite*, in the same tone. Delius conducted its premiére in Oslo. The audience booed, hissed, and eventually cursed at Heiberg's mockery of the Norwegian parliament.

When they reached the point of Delius's parody of the Norwegian anthem in a minor key, the audience gasped, stomped their feet and rushed the conductor and the orchestra. A pistol was waved, and a shot rang out. The conductor and playwright ran out of the theater's rear exit to the Grand Hotel next door, while the police dealt with the crowd outside.

An elderly gentleman with white sideburns looked at them quizzically until Delius explained what had happened. The gentleman said, "I am sorry for the affront Norway has offered a distinguished visitor, Herr Delius. You must remember we are barbarians up here. Allow me to apologize. I am Henrik Ibsen." When the crowd had settled down, Delius returned to his own hotel, only to be told that he was not allowed to stay there.

In 1913, the premiére of Igor Stravinsky's *Le Sacre du Printemps* at the Theatre des Champs Elysées in Paris caused a near riot. The audience hissed, shouted, and whistled at what they viewed as a affront to traditional music. Pandemonium reigned, but nobody shot at the conductor. Fortunately for Delius, the pistol used to shoot at him was loaded with blanks.

A young German conductor, Fritz Cassirer, offered to conduct Delius's symphony *Appalachia* in London. Delius, who had just met Sir Thomas Beecham, asked if Cassirer could use Beecham's orchestra. Beecham agreed and then sat in the audience and was captivated by Delius's music. Beecham became the most active promoter in England of Delius's work, which was popular in Germany but not in England. The famous conductor included at least one Delius work every year in his programs and, occasionally, used his fortune to pay for performances.

Beecham liked Delius personally in addition to liking his music. He commented on Delius's personal qualities: "Delius in his own way was a complete man, carved by nature in a clear and definable piece out of the rough and shapeless stone of her raw material; a signpost to others on the way of life, a light to those in darkness; and an unfailing reassurance to all those who strive to preserve their faith in those two supreme virtues, honesty and independence."

Beecham was known for his conducting ability, his memory, and his sense of humor. One evening he was conducting an opera in which everything that could go wrong, did. Musicians missed their cues, singers sang off key, and props fell onto the stage. Finally, a young elephant, which was part of the opera story, defecated on the stage. Beecham looked at the odoriferous pile, halted the orchestra, turned around to face the audience and said: "The critics have spoken." He resumed conducting the opera after the stage was cleaned.

Delius worked so hard that it began to affect his health. He was exhausted and did not feel well. In the fall of 1910, Jelka took him to a sanitarium in Germany. Slowly, he began to regain his health. Percy Grainger visited him and suggested that he write music for smaller orchestras that would be less expensive to produce. The results of this suggestion were *On Hearing the First Cuckoo in Spring* and *Summer Night on the River.*

In the spring of 1915, Delius had problems with his eyesight and began to wear thick glasses. The fingers on his right had stiffened. One morning while composing *Hassan*, an Arabian nights story about the Near East, at the piano, the pen fell out of his hand. With difficulty, he picked up the pen with his left hand, but his right hand could not grip the pen. He was listless, and his legs were weak. A homeopathic doctor in the area told him that it was a "lameness that would pass off."

By the summer of 1922, Delius needed two canes to walk. On some days, he could only see large objects that were close to him. Two years later, he had to use a wheelchair. He tried hydrotherapy, electric shock treatments, and hypnotism, but no treatment improved his condition for long. Eventually, he had to be carried everywhere he went by a male nurse, and he virtually lost his sight. His condition slowed his composing, but it did not stop it.

Jelka helped Delius finish *Hassan*; however, she was a painter, not a musician. She was not familiar with orchestration; she made many mistakes, and the score had many erasures. Finishing the work was painful to Jelka as well as to Delius. Obviously, he could not continue to compose music in this fashion. In between working on his own compositions, Percy Grainger helped Delius when he could.

In May 1928, Delius received a letter from a young Yorkshireman, Eric Fenby, who offered to come to Grez to take dictation from Delius to help him in composing his music. Fenby was willing to give up several years of his life and to delay his career to perform what he considered to be his self-imposed duty. Fenby was a hard-working, shy, religious person who wanted Delius's composing to continue; also, he realized that he would receive training that he could not get elsewhere.

Initially, Fenby struggled, and Delius became impatient. Fenby was not fast enough for him. After several months, they evolved a productive way of working together. Delius became a news item. He was referred to as the "blind composer" and the "crippled genius." Newspaper staff writers frequently described his working relationship with Fenby. Fenby described life at Grez:

> There was nothing of the sickly, morbid, blind composer as known by popular fiction here, but a man with a heart like a lion, and a spirit that was as untamable as it was stern. Once you had crossed the threshold of that great door to the street you found yourself in another world—a world, peaceful and self-sufficient, which centered around the figure of Delius. It was a world with its own laws, its own standards of right and wrong, in all things, its own particular sense of beauty and its own music. It had been created for musicmaking.

In January 1929, King George presented Delius with the Order of the Companion of Honor. Delius was proud of the recognition. In the fall of 1929, Sir Thomas Beecham convinced Delius to come to London to hear his music performed in a series of six concerts. Delius was overwhelmed by the fervor of his fans in England. Beecham had prepared well for the concerts, and the concerts were standing room only. Delius was asked to speak after one of the concerts: "Ladies and gentlemen. Thank you for the very fine reception you have given me. It was wholly unexpected. I also wish to thank Sir Thomas Beecham for the inspired manner in which he played my music. This festival has been the time of my life. Again I thank you."

Delius, Jelka, and Fenby returned to Grez, where Delius worked on a sonata. The pressure of working with an elderly person who was ill was taking a toll on Fenby. He was on the verge of a nervous breakdown. He told Delius that he had to go home to England, at least briefly. Fenby returned to Grez early in 1931 to help Delius with his work on *Irmelin*, an opera about a princess who fell in love with a prince who searched for a magic river and a wandering troubadour.

Fenby again was weighed down by his role and had to return to England, where he collapsed from the strain late in 1931. In August 1932, he returned again to Grez to help Delius with *Fantastic Dance,* based on Negro blues music. In the summer of 1933, Fenby left Grez a third time. It was a solitary existence for a young man, and Delius's irritability was difficult to handle.

In January 1933, Delius began to sleep during much of the day. In May 1934, Jelka had an operation for cancer, and Fenby returned to help the nurse care for Delius. Jelka returned from the hospital the following month and was home in Grez on June 10, 1934, when Delius died. The British Broadcasting Corporation released a news bulletin: "We regret to announce the passing of Mr. Frederick Delius, Companion of Honor," accompanied by the playing of "The Walk to a Paradise Garden" from *A Village Romeo and Juliet*. A newspaper headline announced: "MUSIC'S BLIND HERO IS DEAD; HIS SOUL GOES MARCHING ON."

Jelka and Fenby took Delius's body to England for burial in Limpsfield Churchyard, Surrey. Jelka died on May 28, 1935, after contracting pneumonia on the ship crossing the channel.

* * *

Elizabeth Barrett Browning and Robert Browning and Frederick and Jelka Delius are outstanding examples of the importance of relationships in living a productive and happy life. The Brownings are one of the foremost role models of a romantic couple. Their relationship, documented in over 600 letters, is an example of what two people can mean to each other.

As Delius's illness progressed and he became unable to walk and lost his eyesight, he was still able to compose because of Jelka's assistance. Jelka gave up a promising career as an artist to help her husband. Eric Fenby, Delius's assistant, observed "One thing was uppermost in my mind at Grez, and that was that only there, and with such constant care as his wife lavished upon him, could he [Delius] go on living. Her name deserves a very prominent place on the scroll of those who have given themselves unstintingly for others."

CHAPTER 11

TEAMWORK — ROLE MODELS

Alfred Lunt and Lynn Fontanne—Actors

Jayne Torvill and Christopher Dean—Olympic Champion Ice Dancers

"A person's ability to be interpersonally intelligent is really challenged when it comes to teamwork. All of us are involved in some kind of teamwork, whether at work, with another parent, in a neighborhood group, or in a service organization. Being a part of a team is challenging because you have less personal control over the outcome than you might have in a one-to-one relationship. It's often frustrating since you have fewer opportunities to get your point across and persuade others. Working on a team takes special skills, such as complementing the styles of others, coordinating the efforts of team members without bossing them around, and building consensus."

Mel Silberman, *People Smart*

LYNN FONTANNE AND ALFRED LUNT—Actors

"They are strange and wonderful personalities—very difficult to understand until you realize that they are not two, but one personality. Each is the other's complement. Together they are marvelous, their artistry amazing. Apart, they are oddly ineffectual. Alfred, a vaguely wandering soul who looks at you like a lost dog who is afraid of being washed; Lynn—splendidly null, a sort of highly intellectual ice-maiden. Alfred's genius illuminates Lynn; Lynn's strong brain and well balanced judgement keep Alfred within bounds and bring him back to earth when he soars skyward. I love them both, but the Alfred-Lynn combination is the real person, not the component parts."

W. Graham Robertson

Lynn Fontanne and Alfred Lunt, generally considered the premier stage actress and actor during the 1920s, 1930s, and 1940s, were a finely tuned acting team who complemented each other to an incredible degree. They strived for perfection and continually improved a play until its final performance. Occasionally, they would have a disagreement during a rehearsal, but by the end of the performance they would walk away arm in arm.

Each was willing to appear in a play that showcased the other's talents, but was only a light vehicle to display his or her own acting ability. They were teamwork personified, and their acting genius grew the longer they performed together. They spent twenty-four hours a day in each other's company, by choice, and were happily married for over fifty years.

Memories of Lynn Fontanne and Alfred Lunt have begun to fade. Their last Broadway play was *The Visit* at the Lunt-Fontanne Theatre in 1958. Although the Lunts performed in many serious plays, such as *The Sea Gull, Taming of the Shrew,* and *The Visit,* they are remembered mainly as the sophisticated and witty antagonist and protagonist in comedies.

Fontanne and Lunt aren't generally well remembered because they acted only on the stage; they had little exposure in the electronic media. They made one motion picture together, *The Guardsman,* and then rejected all other offers to appear in films. They performed in a few radio shows, which usually were shortened versions of their plays, as a supplement to their stage productions. They didn't perform on television until he was sixty-five and she was seventy, when they were nearing retirement.

Fontanne and Lunt performed in their plays to many audiences on the road but reached only a fraction of the audience they could have reached in films. Both Fontanne and Lunt were born to perform on the stage; neither considered any other career.

Fontanne and Lunt were open with each other when offering constructive criticism of the other's acting; however, it was difficult at first. Fontanne saw an early performance of *The Intimate Strangers*, and Lunt asked her for comments on his performance. She said, "You worked too hard. Act being relaxed." Of this early criticism, Fontanne said, "He didn't like that at all." As they matured as actors, two real strengths were their mutual support and their critical suggestions about each other's acting—feedback that helped improve their acting skills.

In an interview, Fontanne said, "We were two actors being perfectly honest with each other. To an outsider it might have sounded cruel. We didn't sound cruel to each other. It's just that we didn't have to bother with the 'now-darling-of-course-you're-the-most-marvelous-actor-in-the-world-but-there's-just-one-little-thing' beginning. We've always been pretty straight with each other."

Fontanne observed, "Over a long run, you lose your eye and you lose your ear. And I have to keep watch over him as he does over me. And I think that is very possibly one of the reasons, if I might say so, for our success. I think that we are terrifically critical of each other. And we've learned, the both of us, to take it. If [when I'm performing] I'm tired and it gets into my own voice—I hear about it from Alfred. Make no mistake, I hear about it."

In *Stagestruck*, Maurice Zolotow writes: "It took about eight years after Lynn and Alfred were married until they fused into one being, until they were no longer Lunt and Fontanne, but the Lunts; yet the Lunt and the Fontanne remained, separate personalities in the one being. They retained certain temperamental differences."

Fontanne was more stable than her husband. Lunt was vulnerable and continually doubted his abilities as an actor, even after he was highly successful. Frequently, Fontanne would have to jolt him out of his self-doubt with a comment such as, "Oh, Alfred, do stop looking like a horse in a fire."

On one occasion, Fontanne was unwilling to slap her husband hard enough to be realistic. In *At Mrs. Beams*, a light British comedy, Fontanne and Lunt had roles that required them to have a battle royal on the stage. She tries to punch him, but he backs away. She wrestles with him and pushes him over in a chair. They roll over and over on the floor, swinging at each other. The fight scene ends with Fontanne slapping Lunt "hard in the face," but she couldn't bring herself to hit him hard enough.

One afternoon in rehearsal, Lunt pushed his wife away and said, "Lynn, you are the rottenest actress I ever worked with." He turned and walked away, but she grabbed him by the shoulder, turned him around, and slapped him across the mouth so hard his head tilted. Then Lunt folded his arms, smiled, and said, "That's more like it." Fontanne responded, "Alfred, darling, sometimes I think you are a cold-blooded S.O.B." He replied, "Sometimes, I agree with you."

The final version of the fight scene, which lasted twenty minutes, was so realistic that many in the audience gasped. Some theater-goers returned a second and a third time just to see the fight. Arctic explorer Vilhjalmur Stefansson saw the play forty-two times.

The Lunts' arguments were all about acting technique. Their friends could not remember a time, either in their apartment in New York or at their home in Genesee Depot, Wisconsin, when they argued about a personal issue.

Noel Coward described a difference of opinion when they performed in *Design for Living*. "She went up on a line and she refused to admit that she had forgotten it, and she said that Alfred had thrown her off by changing his movements." Fontanne asked Lunt, "Are you going to put down that glass there?" He responded, "I've always put that glass there." She said, "No, you haven't. You put it down here. You're doing it purposely."

The argument elevated to the point Coward thought they were "going to tear each other to shreds." However, the Lunts realized they were behaving unprofessionally and immediately ended their argument. Coward observed that after the rehearsal, "They [walked] out arm in arm as if nothing had happened."

The Lunts owned a triplex on East 63rd Street in Manhattan. The dining room was on the first floor, the bedrooms were on the second floor, and the living room-studio was on the third floor. When memorizing lines for a new play, Fontanne worked on the third floor, and Lunt rehearsed on the first floor. They spoke their lines loudly without disturbing the other. When they were comfortable with their lines, they sat in the same room on wooden chairs with their knees interlocking. They looked into each other's eyes and spoke their lines. When one of them hesitated or spoke the dialogue incorrectly, the other tightened his or her knees together, and they started over.

Director Lawrence Langer once asked an actor and actress in rehearsal to give the scene the same attention to detail the Lunts would give to it. The actress erupted, "How can any other actors expect to play together as well as Alfred and Lynn? They rehearse in bed!" She was right. Lunt admitted, "Miss Fontanne and I rehearse all the time. Even after we leave the theater, we rehearse. We sleep in the same bed. We have a script in our hands when we go to bed."

Fontanne's sister Antoinette thought the explanation for the transformation of her sister from a plain-looking woman to a beautiful woman was "the appreciation of Alfred." Antoinette sincerely believed Lunt recognized Fontanne's beauty long before anyone else did. She was convinced her sister's view of herself was completely changed when she looked at herself through Lunt's eyes.

Fontanne and Lunt often played married or unmarried lovers who fought with each other verbally, physically, or both. Their humor was risqué and sophisticated. Audiences of the 1920s were less tolerant of overt sexual behavior and language than audiences of the 1960s and later. Fontanne and Lunt could get away with erotic love scenes because they were stylish, and because the audience knew they were married. Lunt had definite opinions about roles involving good-natured love scenes on the stage. He thought that audiences in the 1960s didn't enjoy seeing sexual byplay on the stage:

> Some recent playwrights have made sex a dreadful thing. Sex doesn't have to be ghastly. Sex can be most enjoyable. Lynn and I did morally outrageous things on the stage, and we enjoyed it, and the

174

audience enjoyed it because it was gracious and lovely; and most persons have known the happy experience of sex, in marriage usually, as Lynn and I have, but when when one plays comedy, naturally, there is going to have to be a plot and this means there will be some sexual intrigue and infidelity, but it is always in the spirit of pleasure not of tragedy.

During a performance of *Caprice*, one of their love scenes was so steamy an elderly matron squirmed and started to leave her seat and the theater. Her companion, another respectable older woman, took her by the arm and urged her to stay while whispering, "Isn't is nice, my dear, to know that they really are married."

Fontanne and Lunt met in the late spring of 1919 at the New Amsterdam Theatre, when they starred in *Made of Money*. Lunt was already on stage when Fontanne arrived for the first rehearsal. She sat in the wings next to Sidney Toler, who later became popular in films as Charlie Chan. Fontanne watched and listened to Lunt and was impressed by his manner and his voice. Toler told her: "That young man's voice is literally a gift from heaven. A voice like that can't be acquired. You have to be born with it."

Lunt had earlier seen Fontanne in *Wooing of Eve* and considered her a fine actress; however, he had not thought about her romantically. A year and a half later, as he hurried off stage to meet his leading lady, he was captivated by her. He immediately became awkward and didn't know what to say. While attempting to impress Lynn, he made a sweeping bow and reached for her hand to kiss it. However, he was standing at the head of a short flight of stairs; he lost his balance and fell backward down the stairway. Playwright George S. Kaufman, who was known for his wry humor, later commented, "Well, he certainly fell for her."

Lunt wasn't injured in the fall. Later, he said, "I was so exhilarated and happy as though I had been drinking champagne." Fontanne thought the fall was "prophetic," both in terms of falling for each other, and because Lunt's confident manner masked shyness and uncertainty. Fontanne told actress Laurette Taylor she was in love with Lunt, and Lunt confided to playwright Robert E. Sherwood he was deeply in love with Fontanne.

When the company moved to Washington, D.C., for the opening of *Made of Money,* Fontanne and Lunt spent every waking moment together and often took long rides in Rock Creek Park. They received excellent reviews; however, Fontanne's reviews were more glowing than Lunt's. At this stage of their careers, her craft was more developed than his.

Lunt's mother was not convinced Fontanne was the right woman for her son. Harriet Sederholm visited him in New York to restate her reservations while Fontanne was on tour. When Fontanne returned to New York, Lunt was torn between loyalty to his mother and love for his co-star. Fontanne and Lunt argued about his mother's influence over him; he went to Philadelphia to escape his worries in New York.

Fontanne turned to Laurette Taylor for advice. Of Fontanne, Taylor said, "a more miserable pup you never saw." Taylor said the situation was serious and advised her to track down Lunt in Philadelphia to resolve their disagreement. Fontanne did; Lunt was pleased and relieved to see her. They patched up their differences, and Lunt said he wouldn't let his mother come between them.

When Fontanne and Lunt returned to New York, their relationship cooled down again. Taylor didn't know what had happened but noticed Fontanne "seemed doubly hurt. One difference was she no longer wanted to talk about Lunt. In fact you could imagine that no such person as Mr. Lunt had ever met Miss Fontanne." Taylor advised Fontanne to forget Lunt and find someone else. When his mother returned to Wisconsin, Lunt telephoned Fontanne to ask her forgiveness. They went out to dinner and reconciled.

Fontanne remembered that dinner. "What a day that was. My, but we had a high old dinner together celebrating, and we were so happy. I didn't think I'd ever be that happy again. I didn't care if I ever acted in another play again. Just having Alfred back in my arms was all I wanted."

In 1919, when Lunt played in *Clarence,* the five female characters all loved the hero of the play. The plot was true offstage as well; the actresses who played the women's parts all loved Lunt. Nineteen-year-old Helen Hayes was one of them. Hayes's mother knew Helen "was carrying a secret passion in her heart for Alfred." Hayes was "certain this bony, brazen woman [Fontanne] was not for him" and wondered when he would extricate himself from this "sophisticated hussy." Each night after the curtain closing of *Clarence*, Fontanne sauntered into Lunt's dressing room and stayed while he dressed. Then, arm in arm, they left the theater. Actress Mary Boland thought it "most unseemly for a single female to be going into Lunt's dressing room." Later, Boland tried to talk Lunt out of marrying Fontanne.

Helen Hayes had even stronger feelings about Fontanne than Boland had. To her, Fontanne was "Eliza Doolittle come to life. Seldom have I seen a more awkward, skinny creature. I squirmed with jealousy and resented her fiercely. I derived some satisfaction from knowing the cast felt she tried to impress us as she paraded in front of our hostile eyes." Later, Fontanne admitted, "I could feel it you know; I could feel the daggers right between my shoulder blades."

Hayes was in love with Lunt for several years, until she encountered playwright Charles MacArthur at a party. MacArthur, who had not yet met Hayes, saw her across the room. He walked over to her, offered her a bowl of salted peanuts, and said, "I wish these were emeralds." Hayes had met the man of her dreams, and it was easy to forget Lunt. Subsequently, Hayes and MacArthur were married.

Lunt and Fontanne moved into a theatrical boarding house on West 70th Street. Fontanne had a suite on the third floor, and Lunt had a room in the basement. It was a romantic time for them. They strolled in Central Park, rode double-decker buses on Fifth Avenue, and watched ships in New York harbor from a bench in Battery Park. Playwright Noel Coward came to New York from London and visited them in the brownstone on 70th Street. Later, Coward remembered the plans they made:

> From these shabby, congenial rooms, we projected ourselves into future eminence. Lynn and Alfred were to be married. That was the first plan. Then they were to become definitely idols of the public. That was the second plan. Then this all successfully accomplished, they were to act exclusively together. This was the third plan. It remained for me to supply the fourth, which was that when all three of us had become stars of sufficient magni-

tude to be able to count upon an individual following irrespective of each other, then, poised serene-
ly upon that enviable plane of achievement, we
would meet and act triumphantly together.

Fontanne and Lunt succeeded with that plan while still young.
Early in their careers, they performed in separate plays, frequently
in different cities. Then they insisted on at least performing in the
same city. When they achieved stardom, they only performed
together because they were the most successful actress and actor
performing for the Theatre Guild, which could guarantee a play's
success by including them in the cast. The final phase of their plan
with Coward was implemented when they appeared in his plays,
beginning with *Design for Living*.

Fontanne and Lunt delayed getting married for economic reasons. He sent money home to help his mother with the expenses of
raising his stepsisters and stepbrother. Finally, they set May 27,
1922, as their wedding date. On the morning of the 26th, Lunt
became impatient. They were sitting on a bench in Central Park
when he said, on the spur of the moment, "Let's get married! Now!
Immediately!" Since the wedding was to be a small civil wedding
anyway, he asked her why wait another day.

Fontanne and Lunt took the subway to City Hall and asked who
could marry them. Deputy City Clerk James J. McCormick agreed
to perform the ceremony and asked where their witnesses were.
Two employees from the city clerk's office agreed to serve as witnesses in the chapel of the Municipal Building. An embarrassed
Fontanne and Lunt realized they had no money to pay for the wedding license, so they borrowed the fee from the witnesses.

Later in life, the Lunts used a short piece of repartee when they
were being honored and in interviews:

> He: In all our years together there has never been one
>   thought of divorce.
> She: Oh, no, never.
> He: Murder, yes!
> She: Yes!
> He: But never divorce.

Fontanne and Lunt did everything together and were not comfortable apart. In 1930, Lunt went for a walk and stopped to visit a friend for a half hour. It was just before dinnertime, and the friend asked if he would like to go to dinner with him. Lunt was aghast. "Without Lynn?" he asked. He grabbed his hat and hurried home.

Noel Coward had learned this about Fontanne and Lunt early in their friendship. Initially, Coward tried to determine whether he enjoyed the company of one more than the other. One day he experienced an epiphany—Fontanne and Lunt weren't two separate people. Coward said, "They were one person and now I realized why I'd never been able to decide between them."

In the mid-1960s, their friend Alan Hewitt experienced an example of their closeness:

> Alfred called me around 6:30 or 7:30 in the evening and said, "Are you doing anything for dinner?" and I said, "Well, I was just going about to fix something for myself here." He said, "Would you do me a great favor? We've got so much food here, and I'd like you to help me with it. Lynn has fallen and broken her arm you see, and I've taken her to Doctors' Hospital. So we have all of this perfectly good food here, and she's not here to eat it. Would you come up and share it with me?" So I said, "Of course." And so I went up to have dinner with him.

> Alfred offered me a drink, and then said, "Now, before we have dinner, if you don't mind, I'm just going to run over and see Lynn." So he went over to Doctors' Hospital, which was just a block away. When he came back, the cook served dinner, and before dessert Alfred said, "I'm sorry, Alan, but I've got to make sure that Lynn's all right. You don't mind, do you?" And back he went to the hospital. Well, that evening, he went there four times! And as I was leaving, he said, "Why don't I walk part of the way with you? It'll give me a chance to stop at the hospital and see how Lynn is doing."

Fontanne once surprised English friends with her response to an invitation. Lady Juliet Duff asked Fontanne to have lunch with her and Lady Cynthia Asquith. Fontanne replied, "I couldn't, I'm afraid, unless you ask Alfred too. I don't go anywhere without him." The ultimate anecdote about their togetherness occurred when Fontanne was asked by the Duchess of Windsor, "Is it true that you and your husband sleep in separate bedrooms?" She replied, "Alfred and I don't even sleep in separate beds."

One reason for their closeness was they didn't have the usual division between work and personal lives but experienced everything together. Noel Coward often wondered whether they acted so well together because they loved each other so much, of if they loved each other so much because they acted so well together. He observed, "Sometimes I've thought that they are in the theater so intensely because the theater makes it possible for them to be together more often and in more ways than they might be if they were in some other line of work."

When asked what had kept them together, Fontanne answered that she remembered admiring Lunt's voice and acting technique the first time they met. She fell madly in love with him and was intoxicated with his presence from then on. She concluded: "I suppose it is rather unusual but there it is."

Lunt's response to the same question was: "People always want to know why we get on so well together and the answer is I've never been bored. She's the most exciting person I've ever known, and I'm in love with her. Married life is spending all your time with a charming person who makes life more interesting because you can spend so much time with her." Fontanne was once asked what was the basis of the strength of their marriage. She replied that it was a mutual respect for each other's privacy. She added:

> I think we're an utter necessity for each other. Neither Alfred nor I dislikes solitude. We like each other's company, but we also cherish our own privacy. We can both be here in the house together and yet not be side by side, just aware of our presences. Alfred can be in the garden all morning while I'm going about my own affairs. Neither Alfred nor I is possessive. Nor do we take from the

other. We're incurious about the other's privacy.
We don't open each other's mail. We have our own
bank accounts. We split all house expenses and we
each pay for our own clothes and medicines and
doctors and I pay for my own maid. Consequently,
we don't have any serious arguments over money.

On their twenty-eighth wedding anniversary, the Lunts were
asked how they had remained happily married for nearly thirty
years. They replied:

We always have been careful to separate our personal and our professional lives. We are together
practically all the time offstage; once we enter the
stagedoor we are like polite strangers. There is no
visiting between dressing rooms. We have work to
do until the curtain falls at eleven o'clock. After
that we always resume our other life and generally
go straight home. When we spend our summer holidays on our farm in Wisconsin, we are careful to
give each other plenty of time to be alone to devote
to separate interests [decorating and sewing for
her, cooking and gardening for him].

On the other hand, we are fortunate also in liking
the same people, so that our friends are always
mutually welcome. Neither of us is much of a par-
tygoer. Many of our friends are outside the theater
as well as in it. We like nothing better than having
a quiet dinner together, and we never have come to
that unfortunate state in which you "run out of
conversation" which sometimes happens to people
who have been married a quarter of a century.

Because of their closeness, Fontanne's and Lunt's friends were
worried about the surviving spouse when one of them died, particularly if Lunt outlived Fontanne; they considered him less able to
handle the grief. Lunt passed away on July 21, 1977; Fontanne died
in her sleep on July 30, 1983.

Several years after Lunt's death, an interviewer asked Fontanne, "With all the triumphs and accolades you've received through the decades, what was the real highlight?" Without hesitation, Fontanne replied, "My marriage to Alfred—I miss him every second of every day."

JAYNE TORVILL AND CHRISTOPHER DEAN—Olympic Champion Ice Dancers

"How successfully a team functions is directly related to how effectively the members communicate with one another in group situations. We've all been in meetings that seem magical: you could almost feel an electric energy as people share ideas, revise suggestions, support one another with enthusiasm, come up with creative and collaborative solutions, and leave feeling that each member of the team is invaluable. Someone uses emotional intelligence to keep the meeting on a positive, forward-moving track. Although it's usually the team leader who is responsible for guiding the tone and the direction of the meeting, the responsibility is shared by each individual, because this is what teamwork is all about."

Hendrie Weisinger, *Emotional Intelligence at Work*

Torvill's and Dean's view of their teamwork from *Torvill & Dean: The Autobiography of Ice Dancing's Greatest Stars:*

At the heart of the relationship is trust. It grew from the earliest days of working together, from our own commitment and reliability, tried and tested time and time again. For the present and immediate future, the commitment is total.

Trust is the foundation. But in practice, the relationship has its complexities and conflicts. Chris is a strict timekeeper, whatever the circumstances; Jayne is the relaxed one. She'll never be early if she can help it.

Jayne is annoyed by Chris's niggling. We'll be coming off the ice after a good performance, usually with Chris leading, and Jayne will hear him say over his shoulder: "I don't know about this step, or such-and-such a lift." Niggle, Niggle, there's always something. She dismisses the remark with "Mm, yeah, sure." Or if he insists: "Can't stop. Got to change." Or she pretends she never heard.

But these are routine annoyances. They have no effect on the underlying trust, or on the qualities that make the relationship work. Instinctively, automatically, we support each other. If anyone else dares to accuse Chris of being undiplomatic, Jayne cuts in with, "What do you mean he shouldn't have said it? He was cross! Why shouldn't he say it?"

We complement each other. If Chris is the creative force, never satisfied with what we've achieved, always pushing for more, needing more, *kneading* more, Jayne is the clay, moulding herself to his ideas, understanding the aims, responding, and interpreting.

After all the years together, we have built up a shorthand way of working. Chris will say something like, "Lay into me, back inside-outside edge." It might mean nothing to another skater, but she'll know it and do it. He's the artist, sketching a vision in words; she sees it and makes it instant reality while he follows a train of thought, suggesting and coaching, she watches and remembers.

That's the role she's happy with. She never wanted to be the leader, she'd rather stay in the background and deal with whatever comes at her. Any expressions of impatience from Chris—and there are a few sometimes after hours of work on steps that don't come out right—bounce right off her. Close friends call her "the Rock."

Emotionally, that's how it works. But physically, when we are together on the ice, the roles are often reversed. If you add up how many turns Jayne has, you would see that she is often the more active one, Chris the rock.

But it is not that she merely does what she's told or ignores him when it suits her. Often, she rules from behind. She responds to the music as much as he does, and if she disagrees with something, if she feels that it really is not going to work, she can see why, and thinks, "If I do that, I won't be able to get out of it elegantly." Then she tells him, and shows him.

"See, it won't work."

"Oh, right."

Sometimes, the exchange happens so quickly that anyone else would miss the glance between us. Often, in anything concerned with skating, we know each other's reactions at once. When we talk, it's usually about skating, and we constantly interrupt each other to finish off each other's thoughts.

We stay together only by sticking to a self-disciplined regime. The rules are quite simple and very demanding. Commitment, hard work, attention to detail. Those are the elements that focus us.

* * *

Alfred Lunt and Lynn Fontanne provide us with an outstanding example of how teamwork and closeness in their professional lives can turn the work of two performers into incredible actors. This teamwork overflowed into their personal lives as man and wife. It is difficult to find a better example of two people working and living as one.

Jayne Torvill and Christopher Dean became olympic ice dancing champions through teamwork and understanding each other thoroughly. Dean was usually the creative force, but, on many occasions, Torvill made creative suggestions that were taken. Their working relationship allowed Torvill to observe that certain moves suggested by Dean would not work, with no hard feelings.

Lunt and Fontanne and Torvill and Dean also had to learn how to work well with the teams producing their plays and performances.

PART II

INDIVIDUALS WHO WERE IN NEED OF PEOPLE SMARTS

Part II provides five role models from history that illustrate undervalued individuals who had accomplished significant things but who were unable to sell their ideas or inventions. Several of them ultimately met with success after much delay and frustration. For some of them, credit was never fully received for their achievements.

Chapter 12 —John Atanasoff, Inventor of the Computer

Chapter 13—Robert Goddard, Rocketry Pioneer

Chapter 14—Developers at Palo Alto Research Center, Xerox

Chapter 15—Reginald Mitchell, Developer of the Spitfire

Chapter 16—Chester Carlson, Inventor of Xerography

"Success is not a quantum leap. It is an accumulation of small changes resulting from perseverance, self-discipline, and learning to get the most from your Emotional Intelligence. . . . The question of why some people have become successful, while others struggle throughout their lives and achieve little, has always fascinated mankind. During most of the twentieth century, we were led to believe that it was our cognitive intelligence, our IQ, that determined how well we would do in life. Yet, our common sense and simple power of observation tells us that this simply cannot be the case—that there must be more to success than how well we do in exams in school."

Harvey Deutschendorf, *The Other Kind of Smart*

CHAPTER 12

John Atanasoff (1903- 1995) Inventor of the Computer

"One night in the late 1930s, in a bar on the border of Illinois and Iowa, a professor of physics at Iowa State College had an idea. After a frustrating day performing tedious mathematical computations in his lab, John Vincent Atanasoff realized that a combination of the binary number system and electronic switches, together with an array of capacitors on a moving drum to serve as memory, could yield a computing machine that would make his life—and the lives of similarly burdened scientists—easier. Then he went back and built the machine in the basement of the physics building. It worked. The whole world changed."

Jane Smiley, *The Man Who Invented the Computer*

John Vincent Atanasoff was born on October 4, 1903, the son of Bulgarian immigrants. Atanasoff's father, a graduate of Colgate University, worked as an industrial engineer in New York and New Jersey before moving the family to Brewster, Florida. Young John was a precocious student, with practical interests as well, such as repairing his father's Model T Ford. After graduating from high school, he worked for a year and taught math classes to earn money for college.

Atanasoff was creative from his youngest days. In *Explaining Creativity,* R. Keith Sawyer cites the traits of creativity: self-confidence, independence, high energy, willingness to take risks, above-average intelligence, openness to experience, and preference for complexity. Atanasoff displayed all of these qualities in addition to what Sawyer describes as "problem finding"—the ability to productively formulate a problem so that the terms of the problem lead to the solution.

Atanasoff majored in electrical engineering at the University of Florida. When he graduated in 1925, he had the highest grade point average up until that time at the university. He applied for master's programs in physics, his first love. Iowa State was the first to reply with an offer of admission and aid. Later, he was accepted for graduate study at Harvard, but he had already been accepted by Iowa

187

State. In addition to taking graduate courses, Atanasoff also taught undergraduate math courses.

Atanasoff met Lura Meeks, an undergraduate student at Iowa State. She had grown up on a farm in Cheyenne, Oklahoma. She was intelligent, energetic, and enterprising. They were married when he received his master's degree in physics in June 1926.

Atanasoff accepted a position teaching mathematics and physics at Iowa State while taking additional graduate physics courses to prepare himself for doctoral studies at the University of Wisconsin, which he began in the winter of 1927. He specialized in quantum mechanics, the science that predicts what happens in systems. His professor of quantum mechanics was John Hasbrouck Van Vleck, who was to win the Nobel Prize in 1977.

Atanasoff's theoretical physics dissertation was "The Dielectric Constant of Helium." Dielectric constant is a practical measurement, the ratio of the electric field in a vacuum to the electric field in a medium. Obtaining solutions to the linear equations that he required was laborious and time consuming.

Atanasoff got his Ph.D at the University of Wisconsin in July 1930. He accepted a position as assistant professor of mathematics and physics at Iowa State. After committing to the position, he was offered a job at Harvard, which he again turned down. He was a gifted teacher who engaged his students in discussions and questioned them to determine their areas of knowledge and ignorance.

Most calculators in 1920 were analog, not digital. Atanasoff read about the Differential Analyzer, developed at MIT in 1927-31 by Vannevar Bush. At Harvard, Howard Aiken was looking for a way to improve the 1822 Difference Engine of Charles Babbage, which had never really worked. Babbage later designed an Analytical Engine using gears and shafts, with which he tried to accomplish too much by building a universal machine.

Aiken attempted to update Babbage's ideas with modern techniques, including using a power supply and electric motor for driving the machine, and master control panels controlled by instructions on punched rolls of paper tape synchronized with the machine along with manual adjustments for controlling the calculation of functions. It used a decimal (base ten) numbering system.

Aiken was driven to develop a calculating machine that could solve differential equations. His doctoral dissertation at Harvard was "Theory of Space Charge Conductions." It was similar to Atanasoff's dissertation in that it considered the properties of vacuum tubes—devices in which electric currents pass through a vacuum between two metal electrodes. The simplest vacuum tube was a diode in which a cathode is heated, releasing negatively charged electrons that flow to a positively charged anode.

Atanasoff wrestled with a number of approaches to building a calculating machine. By the winter of 1937, he knew that whatever design he chose, it had to separate memory from computation. All of his design ideas were unsuccessful, and "I was in such a mental state that no resolution was possible. I was just unhappy to an extreme degree." He knew that he had to get away at least briefly. He got in his new Ford V8 and drove east, with no destination in mind, until he was across the Mississippi River in Rock Island, Illinois, 189 miles from home.

Atanasoff noticed a tavern sign and went in and ordered a drink. As he waited for his drink, the general design of his computing machine came to him as a logical whole. He began to visualize how the component pieces would come together. For several hours he thought about his design, particularly how the memory would work and how an electronically based on-off (binary) system would calculate. Specifically, he pondered the working of the calculator's "regenerative memory"—the mechanism by which capacitors and vacuum tubes would charge one another in a feedback loop.

In 1938, Atanasoff worked on theoretical and practical aspects of four related ideas that he had thought of in the tavern in Illinois:

1. Electronic logic circuits that performed a calculation by turning on and off
2. A binary numbering system, using only 0 and 1 to indicate off and on
3. Capacitors for regenerative memory, which can store electrical charge while not connected to a source
4. Computing by direct logical action, not by enumeration, that is, by counting rather than measuring; the numbers represented by 1s and 0s, the on-off states of the vacuum tubes, which would directly be added and subtracted

In March 1939, Atanasoff submitted an application for a grant of $650 to attempt to build a calculator. In May, his request was granted: $200 for materials and $450 to pay for a student assistant.

Atanasoff was fortunate in obtaining the services of Clifford Berry as his assistant. Berry was knowledgeable, enthusiastic, and enterprising. He combined an exceptional intelligence and mechanical ability with a strong work ethic. Atanasoff and Berry had a "breadboard" prototype ready to test in October 1939. It incorporated seven innovations:

1. Electronic computing
2. Vacuum tubes as the computing mechanism and operating memory
3. Binary calculation
4. Logical calculation
5. Serial computation
6. Capacitors as storage memory
7. Capacitors attached to a rotating drum that refreshed the power supply of the vacuum tubes to regenerate the operating memory

In January 1940, the construction of the new prototype began. The goal was to focus the design of the machine on the solution of differential equations. The calculator would be able to solve equations containing up to twenty-nine unknowns, three times the number then considered possible with current methods.

Atanasoff and Berry constructed what they called the ABC, the Atanasoff-Berry Computer, in the basement of the physics building. The frame of ABC was seventy-four inches long, thirty-six inches deep, and forty inches tall including casters. Solving twenty-nine linear equations with twenty-nine unknowns took thirty hours with periodic inputs from the operator, but it could be done and done accurately.

In August 1940, Atanasoff completed a thirty-five page manuscript, in which he described the ABC in detail, including a list of nine types of linear algebraic equations a larger machine would be able to solve. He described practical applications in physics, statistics, and technology, ranging from problems of elasticity to quantum physics.

Atanasoff planned to use the manuscript to obtain additional development money—$5,000 was needed for the next phase. Atanasoff made three carbon copies of the original manuscript: one for the research corporation, one for Berry, and one for the patent process that Atanasoff thought the machine was ready for.

In December 1940, Atanasoff attended the annual meeting of the American Association for the Advancement of Science in Philadelphia. He also planned to do some patent research in New York and Washington, D.C. One of the reasons Atanasoff attended this annual meeting was to find out what other inventors were doing.

John Mauchly, a physics professor from Ursinis College in Collegeville, Pennsylvania, gave a talk about correlating weather patterns with solar phenomena. He mentioned that he had developed a calculator, the "Harmonic Analyzer," to do the correlations. He discussed his design and talked about his plans for the future. Although the "Harmonic Analyzer" was an analog machine, he thought the future of computing was electronic (digital).

After Mauchly's talk, he and Atanasoff compared notes on their development efforts. Atanasoff invited Mauchly to Ames to see the ABC. When Atanasoff returned home, he met with college officials to persuade them to hire Richard Trexler, an eminent patent attorney from Chicago to process the patent. Atanasoff sent Trexler a copy of the thirty-five page manuscript describing the ABC.

College president Charles E. Friley and college officials still did not appreciate the value of obtaining a patent, but Atanasoff prevailed. Friley wanted the college to get 90% of the potential profits with nothing for Berry. After six months of negotiations, In July 1941, Friley agreed to giving Atanasoff 50% of the profits, less expenses. Berry would receive 10% of Atanasoff's portion.

Mauchly visited Iowa State for four days in July 1941. Atanasoff was very open with him in discussing the ABC. He was pleased to find someone who was interested in his project. The staff at Iowa State wasn't all that interested. Atanasoff loaned Mauchly a copy of his manuscript on the ABC but would not let Mauchly take a copy back to Philadelphia with him.

Mauchly spent considerable time in the basement of the physics building with the ABC, talking with Berry and others. Mauchly had hands-on access to the ABC and actually helped Berry do a few repairs. He and Atanasoff spent every evening talking about the principles of the ABC. One evening, Mauchly asked Lura for some bond paper and she noticed that Mauchly stayed up late at night with his light on. She suspected that he was copying the thirty-five page manuscript. She was concerned he might be stealing her husband's ideas.

Later, Mauchly claimed that the ABC he viewed in Ames was not a working model. Professor George Snedecor of the Iowa State statistics department noted that he "would send problems over to Atanasoff and the ABC would solve them. Then the secretary would check the results on a desktop calculator. And they would be correct." The ABC was in working order.

In the summer of 1941, Mauchly took a course at the Moore School of Electrical Engineering at the University of Pennsylvania. It was a cram course in electronics sponsored by the War Department for scientists in other fields. There he met his future partner, J. Presper Eckert, who had just graduated from the Moore School. Upon completion of the course, Mauchly was invited to join the staff of the Moore School.

Mauchly wrote to Atanasoff to ask, "Is there any objection from your point of view to my building some sort of computer which incorporates some of the features of your machine? In the event that your present design were to hold the field against all challengers, and I got the Moore School interested in having something of the sort, would the way be open to build an 'Atanasoff Calculator' here?"

In September 1942, Atanasoff left Ames for a war-related position at the Naval Ordnance Laboratory in Washington, D.C. Iowa State told Atanasoff that the patent process was well in hand. He left the ABC in the basement of the physics building. Atanasoff worked for the Naval Ordnance Laboratory for the next seven years, during which time he was out of touch with the patent submission at Iowa State. When he inquired about the patent process, he was not given clear answers.

In the spring of 1943, Mauchly visited Atanasoff at the Naval Ordnance Laboratory. He told Atanasoff about a project at the Moore School calculating trajectories of large artillery pieces. Mauchly described how he and Eckert were devising a machine the army could use to make firing-range calculations. In his paper,

"The Use of High-Speed Vacuum Tubes for Calculation," Mauchly described "an electronic device operating solely on the principle of counting" It would do the same tasks as an analog device but would do them faster.

The Moore School began to develop the ENIAC (Electronic Numeric Integrator and Computer). When it was finished, it weighed twenty-seven tons, and was eight feet long, eight feet high, and three feet deep. It had 18,000 vacuum tubes, 7200 diodes, 1,500 relays, and 10,000 capacitors for memory storage. It was not programmable.

Atanasoff met mathematician John von Neumann when he visited the Naval Ordnance Laboratory. Von Neumann wrote a paper describing a second version of ENIAC, "First Draft of a Report of the EDVAC, by John von Neumann." EDVAC stood for "Electronic Discrete Variable Automatic Computer." The paper described "Von Neumann architecture," in which the computer would contain a set of instructions in its memory, that is, it would be programmable.

In February 1946, Atanasoff attended the unveiling of ENIAC at the University of Pennsylvania; neither Mauchly nor Eckert were present. He didn't learn much about the principles of the machine. He called Richard Trexler, the Chicago patent attorney, and was told that his patent was never filed because Iowa State had never paid the filing fee.

Another ongoing computer development project at the time was Howard Aiken's Mark I at Harvard, which was built by IBM, the supplier of the punched-card system for ENIAC. In the spring of 1946, Mauchly and Eckert formed their own company. Mauchly's responsibility was to manage the company and to obtain financing and contracts. Eckert was in charge of building the first UNIVAC (Universal Automatic Computer), which became available in March 1951.

The IBM 701 was announced in April 1952, followed by the 702, the 650, and the 705. The 701 and the 650 were designed for business use. Two of IBM's advantages were the punched-card systems in widespread use and the fact that IBM rented their machines.

Filmmaker Kirwin Cox noted that the EDVAC design was closer to the ABC design than the ENIAC configuration and that ENIAC was a hybrid machine—partially ABC, partially Bush Analyzer, and partially ganged calculators. Cox also observed: "John Vincent Atanasoff was a lucky man in many ways. He lived to see his hard work and enterprising intelligence vindicated. He spent a long life trying many things and, because of his energy, organizational skills, and and persistence, mastering everything he tried." Cox called him the "lone inventor" type, who explores and invents and then exhausts his interests in a given idea.

* * *

Atanasoff could have spent considerably more effort protecting his ideas, particularly, in not being so open and in following up on his patent application process. Admittedly, he was busy at the Naval Ordnance Laboratory during the war years. Nevertheless, he should have been willing to spend the time to ensure that he received credit for his work. However, Cox noted of Atanasoff, "Money and fame are secondary to passionate curiosity."

CHAPTER 13

Robert Goddard (1882-1945) Rocketry Pioneer

"As I looked toward the fields in the East I imagined how wonderful it would be to make some device which had even the possibility of ascending to Mars, and how it would look on a small scale if sent up from the meadow at my feet. I was a different boy when I descended the tree from when I ascended, for existence at last seemed very purposive."

Robert Goddard

On October 19, 1899, at age seventeen, Goddard climbed a large cherry tree in the backyard of his home to prune dead branches with a saw and hatchet. He had recently read H. G. Well's *War of the Worlds*, which at least partially explains the significant emotional event that occurred. He climbed down from the tree and made the above entry in his diary.

The realization that "for existence at last seemed very purposive," was a great motivator for Goddard's subsequent endeavors. He felt that he now had a purpose in life and a goal to "somehow make something that would go higher than anything had before." Every year for the remainder of his life, he viewed October 19 as his "Anniversary Day."

Goddard began his research with rockets as an undergraduate at Worchester Polytechnic Institute and as a graduate student at Clark University. While recovering from an illness in 1913, he worked on rocket designs. During this time, he applied to the United States Patent Office for the first two of approximately 200 patents he was granted in his lifetime. His first patent described the characteristics required by all modern rockets: a combustion chamber with a nozzle, a pump to force fuel into the combustion chamber, and the propellant, either solid or liquid, which burns in the combustion chamber.

Goddard's second patent outlined the concept of the multistage rocket that is the forerunner of the high-altitude rockets in use today. Earlier, Goddard investigated the efficiency of rocket fuel. A simple rocket using gunpowder placed in a cylinder closed at one end and ignited uses only about two or three percent of the energy of the fuel. Goddard's two principal goals were to improve the basic design of the rocket and to develop an improved rocket propellant.

By the fall of 1914, he was well enough to resume work on a part-time basis on the faculty of Clark University. Within a year, he had built some of the rockets that he had designed. He developed a nozzle design to improve the propellant efficiency and to generate more thrust. By the summer of 1915, working with solid fuel rockets, he had achieved a fuel efficiency of forty percent and was recording ejection velocities of 6,700 feet per second. After many partial successes, he launched a rocket that reached a height of 486 feet and had an ejection velocity of just under 8,000 feet per second.

Goddard realized that he could not afford to continue his research on his own. He wanted to begin his experiments with liquid fuels and he knew that the effort would be costly. He wrote a paper to describe his rocket theory, the mathematics that supported it, and his expectations for further development. He forwarded his paper, entitled "A Method of Reaching Extreme Altitudes," to several scientific institutions to promote interest in his endeavors.

The Smithsonian Institution, whose stated propose is the increase of knowledge among men, was one of the institutions to which he sent his paper. In his letter to the Smithsonian, he wrote, "I have reached the limit of the work I can do singlehandedly, both because of the expense and also because further work will require more than one man's time." Goddard and the Smithsonian scientists felt that it would be useful for meteorologists to have additional knowledge of the atmosphere hundreds of miles from the earth's surface.

The Smithsonian Institution decided to support Goddard's projects. Goddard provided the status of his development effort to the Smithsonian on a regular basis. In one of his communications, he mentioned the potential usefulness of rockets in war time. When the United States declared war in 1917, Dr. Abbott of the Smithsonian passed on Goddard's suggestions to the U.S. Army Signal Corps.

Goddard left his teaching position at Clark University and began working on a hand-held rocket to be used by the U.S. Infantry against enemy tanks. A successful demonstration was conducted in the fall of 1918 at the Aberdeen Proving Grounds in Maryland. It appeared that this weapon, the forerunner of the World War II bazooka, would be put into immediate production. However, with the signing of the armistice on November 11, 1918, the U.S. Army suspended their interest in rockets for over twenty years.

Goddard returned to Clark University and evolved his designs for nose cones, combustion chambers, and nozzles; he also investigated liquid fuels. He realized early that liquid hydrogen and liquid oxygen would be an optimum fuel. However, liquid hydrogen was very difficult to manage, so he searched for a substitute. He chose gasoline since it was inexpensive and relatively dependable. Handling liquid oxygen was problematical since its boiling point is 298 degrees below zero Fahrenheit, and it had to be kept under pressure.

Goddard conducted tests of his liquid fuel rockets at a farm owned by a family friend. The first liquid fuel rocket flight occurred March 16, 1926. It reached a height four times its length and a speed of sixty miles an hour while traveling a distance of 220 feet. He had to redesign the original rocket because the combustion chamber burned through due to the intense heat. Use of sheet steel was a temporary solution to the problem. He experimented with increasingly large rockets, and he added a thermometer and a barometer as well as a small camera to record the instrument readings.

In July 1929, Goddard had his most successful flight to date. The rocket gained an altitude of ninety feet and traveled 171 feet in its eighteen and one half seconds of flight. As he and his associates were picking up the reusable pieces of the rocket, the crash site was visited by an ambulance, several police cars, and cars with signs marked "Press." They had received a report of an airplane crash. This incident gave the rocket experiments bad press. The Smithsonian Institution supported Goddard by explaining that he was attempting to collect weather information at high altitudes. Commonwealth officials would not allow any more experimental rocket flights to be conducted in Massachusetts.

Goddard and his assistants looked for a more compatible location to resume rocket testing. They considered the amount of rainfall, topological features, and general climate conditions. They chose Roswell, New Mexico, for future tests. In addition to the favorable climate, the area around Roswell was sparsely settled and met their criterion of having few neighbors to become alarmed by the noise of their experiments.

The first major test at the Roswell site was in December 1930. The purpose was to see if compressed nitrogen gas from an outside tank could be used, when routed through tubes to the fuel and oxidizer tanks, to force gasoline and liquid oxygen into the combustion chambers. In this successful flight, the rocket reached a speed of 500 miles per hour and an altitude of two thousand feet and traveled 1,000 feet from the launch tower.

Goddard experienced continuing problems with the burning through of the narrow opening between the combustion chamber and the nozzle. He tried different metals but finally concluded that the walls of the combustion chamber needed cooling. He solved this problem using by curtain cooling. He developed a design in which gasoline was sprayed on the inner wall of the combustion chamber prior to its ignition.

In effect, Goddard placed a layer of burning gas around the inside of the combustion chamber that, because it was cooler than the burning gasoline and oxygen in the center of the chamber, resulted in the necessary cooling. In future tests, the problem of burned-through rocket engines was reduced considerably. He also experimented with placing parachutes in the nose cones to lessen damage to the rockets as they returned to earth.

On April 19, 1932, Goddard conducted his first test of a rocket equipped with a gyroscope to control the guidance vanes of the rocket. These adjustable vanes were used to keep the rocket on a vertical course longer than had been possible previously. Also, the gyroscope was used to release the parachute as the rocket approached its maximum altitude. The Guggenheim Foundation, which supported Goddard's research when the need for funds exceeded the amount provided by the Smithsonian Institution, was unable to provide the support for the years 1933 and 1934. Goddard returned to Worchester and resumed teaching at Clark University. Resumption of the support from the Smithsonian Institution allowed Goddard to continue his design efforts.

Goddard's most significant development during his time back in Worchester was a combustion chamber in which atmospheric air was used as the oxidizer. Obviously, this would not work for a high altitude rocket, but it worked for a rocket that traveled horizontally at low altitudes. This type of rocket could be much lighter than a high altitude rocket since it would not have to carry a tank of liquid oxygen.

Goddard used a funnel as the air intake at the front of the rocket motor. The air passed by a shutter-type intake valve on its way to the combustion chamber. The air came in while the shutters were open, the shutters closed, and combustion occurred, providing the thrust. Then the shutter opened and the process was repeated over again. This concept was used by the Germans on their V-1 rocket in World War II. The air resonance noise of the shutter opening and closing was the unusual sound that gave the "buzz-bomb" its name.

The Guggenheim Foundation resumed its support of Goddard's work in the fall of 1934. By this point, Goddard had concluded that the current design was too complex, and that it must be simplified to increase reliability. He wanted to eliminate the need for the nitrogen gas and its associated tank and to use centrifugal pumps to force the liquid oxygen and gasoline into the combustion chambers. The size of the tanks and their weight was the main difficulty. Goddard and his associates worked until 1940 to reduce the size and weight of the tanks and pumps.

By 1937, German scientists were performing rocket experiments at a large, liquid-propellant facility at Peenemunde. The Nazi government provided ample financial backing; they had an operational V-2 ready by 1943.

In May 1940, Harry Guggenheim of the Guggenheim Foundation called a meeting of representatives of the Army, the Army Air Corps, and the Navy that provided Goddard an opportunity to present his work and to promote the potential of liquid propellant rockets in time of war. The Army representative stated that the next war, which had already started in Europe, "will be won by trench mortars." The only interest expressed by Army Air Corps and Navy authorities was for a rocket motor to assist short runway take-off of heavily loaded aircraft.

This joint Army Air Corps and Navy project was the first project assigned to Goddard to aid the war effort. Out of this work came the JATO unit, the jet-assisted take-off device that used solid fuel. His next assignment was to develop a rocket motor with variable thrust that could be controlled by a pilot. This engine design was successful; a version of it was used on the X-2 and the X-15 experimental aircraft later. His last assignment was the development of a small liquid oxygen- and gasoline-powered rocket for use in a guided missile.

Despite the fact that Goddard laid out the principles underlying rocket flight and that all modern rockets evolved from concepts developed by him, the United States did not take advantage of his work. Much of Goddard's early rocket design work was available for the asking. Some of it was technical literature available upon request from the Smithsonian Institution. German rocket scientists, including Werner Von Braun, acknowledged openly that their work was based on the earlier efforts of Goddard.

Robert Goddard is example of an individual whose early academic work was not notable, but, once he had a firm goal in mind, he applied himself to achieve that goal. He was motivated to add to his chosen body of knowledge even though he received little recognition for his efforts.

* * *

Goddard attempted to attract interest and publicity for his experiments. Unfortunately, some of the publicity that he attracted was negative. Admittedly, change is frequently difficult—being on what is sometimes referred to as the "bleeding edge." Nevertheless, the results of his experiments were so significant that the U.S. Government should have been harassed about them. Their importance was recognized by the Germans, who used Goddard's findings in their early development of V-1 and V-2 rockets.

CHAPTER 14

Developers at Palo Alto Research Center, Xerox

"The scientists at PARC created more than a personal computer. They designed, built, and used a complete system of hardware and software that fundamentally altered the nature of computing itself. Along the way, an impressive list of digital 'firsts' came out of PARC. In addition to the Alto computer, PARC inventors made the first graphics-oriented monitor, the first hand-held 'mouse' inputting device simple enough for a child, the first word processing program for inexpert users, the first local area communications network, the first object-oriented programming language, and the first laser printer."

Douglas K. Smith and Robert C. Alexander, *Fumbling the Future*

In 1973, over three years before Steve Wozniak of Apple Computer designed and built the Apple I, Xerox's Palo Alto Research Center (PARC) created the first computer dedicated to the use of one person. PARC did more than design and build a computer. Its developers introduced a comprehensive system of hardware and software that changed the environment of computing. PARC called their computer Alto and its environment "personal distributed computing": "personal" because it was designed for use by an individual and "distributed" because it was connected via a network to shared resources, such as printers and other computers.

PARC was unable to convince anyone within Xerox to exploit the technology. PARC was a development and research center, not a manufacturing and marketing organization. The technology languished. Xerox failed to capitalize on their dramatic developments. Apple Corporation promoted the technology and became associated with the introduction of the personal computer. After Apple's initial success, Xerox introduced the Star computer, which was too late and too expensive. Xerox had missed the opportunity.

Xerox established PARC in 1970 as part of the company's plan to acquire or develop digital capability. IBM was entering the copier business, and Xerox knew that they had to expand into the computer business to remain competitive. However, Xerox didn't plan to take on IBM in large mainframe computers. Their goal was to fight it out with IBM in developing products for the "office of the future." In other words, they would develop and market equipment and systems to be used by managers and secretaries as well as by production and sales personnel.

Peter McColough, who had succeeded founder Joe Wilson as CEO of Xerox in 1968, decided to buy and expand an existing computer company rather than form a start-up. He approached Control Data Corporation, Digital Equipment Corporation, and the Burroughs Corporation, but no mutually beneficial agreements could be reached. In 1969, Xerox paid $900 million for Scientific Data Systems (SDS), a California-based company that had sales of $100 million in the previous year. Most of the SDS customers were in technical computing, but McColough planned to reorient his new acquisition to commercial computing markets.

SDS had no independent development laboratory. Jack Goldman, who succeeded John Dessauer as director of research at Xerox in 1968, recommended to McColough that Xerox establish a digital research and development center. McColough approved the request, and a talented team of scientists and engineers was assembled at Palo Alto to provide Xerox with future-oriented digital capability. Goldman chose George Pake, a well-regarded physicist with experience in both academia and industry, to establish and manage the new center.

Both Goldman and Pake believed in hiring highly capable people and then following a "bottom up" rather than a "top down" approach to research. Overall goals were conveyed to the researchers, but it was left up to them to tell their managers what they had to do to accomplish them. After all, development of the "architecture of information" involved in moving to the "office of the future" wasn't immediately obvious to high-level managers.

Pake divided the lab into three components:
- The General Science Laboratory (GSL)—conducted research in physics and other basic sciences
- The Systems Science Laboratory (SSL)—was responsible for broad "systems" research in engineering, information, mathematics, operations, and statistics
- The Computer Science Laboratory (CSL)—focused on computer systems

Pake managed the GSL in addition to the laboratory as a whole. Bill Gunning, who had twenty years of computer science experience, was appointed to manage SSL. Jerry Elkind was selected to head CSL. Elkind had worked for NASA and for the computer consultant that designed ARPANet, the first nationwide computer communications network, for the Advanced Research Projects Administration (ARPA) of the Department of Defense. Bob Taylor, who had served as ARPA's chief administrator of computer funding, was named associate director of CSL.

With the high cost of mainframe computers and minicomputers that cost over $100,000, time-sharing was a popular tool. Many users at different terminals were connected to one central computer and shared its use.

Computers were considered fast and people were considered slow, so this was viewed as a good arrangement. However, it caused many computer scientists to work odd hours, such as the middle of the night, to gain access to the central computer. Developers' schedules were slaves to the computer's schedule. As the cost of computers came down due to the increased use of integrated circuits and microprocessors, an alternative to time-sharing was sought. Taylor recommended a "one computer, one person" solution to the problem.

CSL computer scientist Alan Kay had described a tool called FLEX in his 1969 doctoral dissertation that fit Taylor's concept. It was an interactive tool. "It must be simple enough so that one doesn't have to be a systems programmer to use it, and it must be cheap enough to be owned. It must do more than just be able to recognize computable functions." FLEX was an "idea debugger" and, as such, it was hoped that it was also an "idea media."

Kay proposed that PARC develop a FLEX-like computer called "Dynabook," which he referred to as a "dynamic media for creative thought." When the Dynabook project was turned down by Xerox management, he countered with a project called "interim Dynabook."

Interest in the project began to build within the CSL, and Taylor obtained approval to develop a computer that met the "one person, one computer" criterion. It was called Alto. CSL scientist Butler Lampson described it as having an enhanced display monitor, being virtually as powerful as a minicomputer, operating in a network of distributed machines, and being affordable. He referred to the use of such a computer as "personal computing." Computer scientist Chuck Thacker had some ideas on putting it together. Their goals were to make it both better and cheaper than a minicomputer.

Lampson and Thacker used some of the tools developed by Douglas Englebart, an early advocate of interactive computing, including an input device called a "mouse" and displays that could be divided into multiple "windows." Englebart's mouse was a bulky analog device that was converted into a digital tool and made smaller and more reliable.

Lampson and Thacker planned to improve Englebart's displays. They favored a technique called bit-mapping, which associated each picture element (pixel) with a specific bit of computer memory. Specific binary bits are programmed to be "on "(one) while others are "off" (zero); in combination the bits create a character on the screen and retain it in memory for later use. Unfortunately, this one-to-one relationship of pixels on the screen with bits in the computer's memory required a large storage capacity and was expensive.

Another Alto innovation was multitasking, which allowed one processor to operate as many. A task was performed according to its priority. Multitasking slowed Alto down because the bit-mapped display used the processor two-thirds of the time, but provided more functionality for less cost. In April 1973, after four months of work, the first Alto was completed. Ten Altos were built by the end of the year, and forty were completed by the following summer.

However, hardware alone doesn't make a computer system. Still needed to obtain benefit from the machine were an operating system, programming languages, and application software. As the software became available, three functions were emphasized: communications, printing, and word processing.

The communications tool developed by Robert Metcalfe was called Ethernet, which didn't use telephone lines but relied on local cable runs within a building. Ethernet connected an Alto to shared equipment, such as printers and other Altos. PARC also developed the xerographic laser printer. Laser printers were expensive, but sharing them reduced the cost to individual computer users.

Lampson and CSL scientist Charles Simonyi developed a word processing application called "Bravo," which allowed the word image on the screen to be the same as that which was output by the printer. This feature, which was called "wysiwyg" for "what you see is what you get" wasn't available on earlier word processing packages. Subsequently, a more user-friendly version, called "Gypsy," was developed. Alto was used successfully in an experiment at Ginn & Company, a Xerox textbook publishing subsidiary, to streamline the publishing process.

The Alto effort seemed to be prepared for takeoff. Thacker observed, "It was certainly from my own experience the largest piece of creative effort I have seen anywhere. And it was like being there at the creation. A lot of people worked harder than I have ever seen, or have seen since, doing a thing they all felt was worthwhile, and really thought would change the world." However, no attempt was made to translate PARC's developments into products.

Xerox faced many challenges at the time. In 1972, the Federal Trade Commission (FTC) claimed that the company was monopolizing the plain paper copier market. The FTC accused Xerox of manipulating patent laws, setting prices that were discriminatory, insisting on leases over sales of equipment, and exploiting the market by using joint ownership arrangements with Rank in England and Fuji in Japan. In July 1975, the FTC discontinued the antitrust action. In order to comply with FTC demands, Xerox had to give up its patents, change its pricing policies, and allow supplies such as toner to be sold by other companies.

In late 1973, CEO McColough and president Archie McCardell, a Ford Motor Company financial executive who had joined Xerox in 1971 upon the death of Xerox founder Joseph Wilson, formed a team of four people to plan the future strategy of Xerox. The team was headed by Michael Hughes, who had a corporate planning background, and included George Pake, who had been assigned to corporate headquarters after directing PARC for three years.

The team evaluated four distinct strategies for Xerox and recommended the alternative that pursued the office of the future. They suggested combining computers, copiers, and word-processing typewriters with PARC's innovations in communications, microcircuitry, and software. No action was taken on their recommendation by Xerox management.

Xerox research director Goldman thought that PARC's inventions would be brought to market by SDS. When SDS hemorrhaged financially during the first half of the 1970s, he realized that another avenue would have to be used to capitalize on PARC's innovations. As the emphasis on financial analysis practiced by ex-Ford executives became prevalent at Xerox, Goldman's influence as the senior technical person waned.

In January 1973, Bob Potter became the General Manager of Xerox's Office Products Division, which was responsible for developing and manufacturing office products other than copiers. The division had few successes other than developing a popular facsimile machine. Potter wanted to move the division from Rochester, New York, to another location. Dallas and Silicon Valley were two of the favored locations. Goldman lobbied strongly for Silicon Valley because PARC was located there. However, Dallas was chosen for strictly financial reasons, such as lower costs for labor, taxes, and transportation. The financial types had won again; PARC was to remain isolated from the rest of the company. In Goldman's opinion, this decision had the greatest negative impact of any single decision on the future of digital technology at Xerox.

Potter visited PARC and observed the Alto technology, but decided to concentrate on word processing technology. Although his background was in both technology and operations, he thought that PARC's ideas were too futuristic. Also, he was influenced by the Xerox financial people, who emphasized short-term profits.

PARC was disappointed that the word "software" didn't enter into Potter's plans for Dallas. They thought that products that weren't programmable, such as Potter's electro-mechanical devices, would fail. Within a year and a half of entering the market, Potter's word-processing typewriter was out of date because of its display and communications shortcomings. Xerox's Display Word Processing Task Force recommended that the new word processor be Alto-based. However, a team from Dallas recalculated PARC's estimates for the new product and concluded that the Alto would take longer to build and cost more than the estimates. The task force's recommendation was ignored. Next, Goldman proposed that a small entrepreneurial team be formed to produce a general-purpose workstation using the Alto. That idea was also rejected.

The recession in 1974-75 impacted Xerox. The company found that customers made as many copies in bad times as in good times, but they made them with existing machines. They didn't buy or lease new copiers during a slowed economy. However, the greatest negative impact on Xerox was the staggering loss from the Scientific Data Systems acquisition. Taking on IBM head-to-head in the "office of the future" wasn't working.

Combining the copier and the computer businesses in a functional organization grouped by design and manufacturing, marketing and service, and planning had removed the focus of the computer business. In effect, SDS drifted without a general manager. In July 1975, CEO McColough admitted that the SDS acquisition had been a mistake. No buyer for SDS could be found. Xerox took a write-off of just under $1.3 billion and left the computer business.

In 1975-76, the Office Products Division began to manufacture the laser printer developed at PARC; a patent was received for Ethernet; and the Systems Development Division (SDD) was formed to translate PARC inventions into products. Some PARC-developed products were entering the marketplace. However, Xerox wasn't prepared to exploit the advances made on the Alto.

In 1976, PARC researcher John Ellenby was authorized to produce hundreds of Altos for use with laser printers within Xerox. He thought that at last technology transfer from the lab to the users was beginning to happen. In August 1976, Ellenby submitted a proposal on Alto to the Xerox task force determining new product strategies for the company. No action was taken on his proposal.

Ellenby was pleased when he was asked to organize the 1977 "Futures Day" at which Xerox showcased its new products within the company. His team worked hard and thought that they had made a strong case for proceeding with the Alto. By this time, McCardell had left Xerox to become CEO of International Harvester, and David Kearns from IBM had taken his place as president and chief operating officer. Ellenby was informed that Kearns had decided not to go into production with the Alto.

In 1979, a Xerox investment unit contacted Steve Jobs about investing in Xerox. Jobs requested and received a tour of the PARC facility. Larry Tesler demonstrated Alto for Jobs, who saw its potential immediately. He asked, "Why isn't Xerox marketing this? You could blow everybody away." Once Jobs knew that it could be done, he set out to duplicate it at Apple. He hired Tesler immediately and later Alan Kay, who eventually became an Apple Fellow. Most of the "look and feel" of the Alto that provided its ease of use eventually was incorporated into the Apple Macintosh. Xerox was amazingly open with their technology.

In 1978, Xerox combined the Office Products Division in Dallas with other non-copier units. General Manager Potter left to join McCardell at International Harvester as chief technical officer. In 1979, the Office Products Division was again made independent, and Don Massaro hired from Shugart Associates to be Potter's replacement as General Manager. Massaro, who was known as an entrepreneurial type, announced a new word processor, readied two facsimile machines for the market, announced PARC's Ethernet as a product, and started an electronic typewriter project within the first year. Soon he became interested in Star, a product that had evolved from the Alto.

Massaro asked Xerox management for $15 million to make and sell the Star and was turned down. He scaled down his request and was turned down again. He proceeded on his own using his division's budget. The Star's strength, like Alto's, was its "user interface," including the contents of the screen and the tools provided to work with the display. The Star used icons, action choice menus, and multiple screen windows along with electronic file cabinets, in and out boxes, and wastebaskets. The Star was designed to be used by managers.

Much of the software had already been designed when a decision was made to replace the processor. Hardware is usually designed before software, and compromises had to be made that slowed the speed of the machine to incorporate the new processor. It was the first personal computer to offer the bit-map screen, a laser printer, the mouse, combined text and graphics in the same document, and "what you see is what you get" word processing.

However, it had limitations in addition to its slow speed:
- Because it was a distributed system, it was more expensive than a stand-alone computer. ($16,595 for the workstation, five times the cost of a stand-alone personal computer).
- It didn't offer a spreadsheet.
- Its design was based on a closed architecture, not an open architecture, and suppliers could not make and sell components to be used with it.
- Its programming language wasn't available to the public (only Xerox employees could write application software for it).
- It wasn't compatible with other computers.

In April 1981, the Star was introduced—eight years after the invention of the Alto. It wasn't a successful product; however, the Star (the Xerox 820) was the first personal computer introduced by a Fortune 500 Corporation.

Mishandling the introduction of the personal computer by Xerox was a classic case of missing an opportunity. Unfortunately, the technology developed at PARC was exploited by others and Xerox didn't receive the benefit of its labors. An incredible body of talent had been assembled at PARC during the 1970s. Some of the key people seeded the laboratories of other companies: for example, Charles Simonyi, who was hired by the Microsoft Corporation.

Butler Lampson, Bob Taylor, and Chuck Thacker joined the Systems Research Center of the Digital Equipment Corporation. In 1984, they received the System Software Award from the Association of Computing Machinery for the invention of personal distributed computing. In 1987, President Reagan awarded George Pake the National Medal of Science for the notable accomplishments of PARC.

* * *

The developers at the Palo Alto Research Center of the Xerox Corporation and their failure to capitalize on their user-friendly personal computer design, provide us with an incredible example of lost opportunity. Admittedly, Xerox had some problems at the time receiving national attention that diverted them from adequately evaluating the potential of their development efforts. The fact that PARC was an R & D organization and not a manufacturing or sales organization should not have been an issue. The development team attempted and failed to convince the president of Xerox of the importance of their Alto personal computer on several occasions. One of their few opportunities would have been to continue to browbeat the Board of Directors with their proposal.

CHAPTER 15

Reginald Mitchell (1895-1937) Designer of the Supermarine Spitfire

"Dreamers and doers—the world generally divides men into those two general classifications, but the world is often wrong . . . Dreaming is just another name for thinking, planning, devising—another way of saying that a man exercises his soul. A steadfast soul, holding steady to a dream ideal, plus a steady will determined to succeed in any venture, can make any dream come true. Use your mind and your will. They work together beautifully if you'll only give them a chance."

B. N. Mills

Reginald Joseph Mitchell was born on May 20, 1895, in the village of Talke, Staffordshire. His father was a teacher who later became a school headmaster. At the age of seventeen, Mitchell was apprenticed to Kerr, Stewart, and Company locomotive works at Stoke-on-Trent. He studied mechanics and mathematics as part of his engineering studies in addition to studying drafting in night school. In 1917, he accepted the position of assistant to the chief engineer and designer at the Supermarine Aviation works near Southampton.

Mitchell was married in 1918 and settled in Southampton. In 1920, he was promoted to chief engineer and designer at Supermarine. At the time, most of his projects involved the design of large military flying boats such as the Martlesham Amphibian, for which he won a government prize.

Mitchell established his reputation as an aircraft designer by creating aircraft to compete in the Schneider international seaplane races from 1922 to 1931. The Schneider Trophy race was the world's major aeronautical event. Lieutenant James Doolittle of the U.S. Army was the winner of the race in Baltimore in 1925; he flew a Curtiss biplane on twin floats at an average speed of 232.57 miles per hour. Britain won the Schneider race in 1929 and again in 1930. Britain would become the permanent holder of the Schneider cup with a win in 1931.

Due to the world Depression in the 1930s, government expenditures were significantly reduced. Prime Minister Ramsay MacDonald decided not to finance an entry in the 1931 Schneider cup race. The British public protested strongly. In January 1931, Lady Houston, the wealthy widow of a shipping magnate, contributed £100,000 to finance an entry in the 1931 race. The Supermarine S.6B, winner of the 1931 Schneider Trophy, was an early prototype of the Spitfire fighter aircraft. Thus a private citizen, Lady Houston, was a contributor to the development effort of a high-performance fighter aircraft of World War II.

All of the major design criteria for the evolving Spitfire had been defined by the summer of 1935. Changes to the design incorporated into the final prototype, which was built in the fall of 1935, included a thinner, elliptically shaped wing, ducted radiator cooling, and eight machine guns instead of the four machine guns originally specified.

Unfortunately, the chief designer was able to spend only limited time on the project. In 1933, Mitchell was diagnosed with cancer and underwent an operation. If he had followed his doctor's advice and either taken an extended leave of absence or reduced his efforts, he might have been cured of cancer, or at least have extended his life. However, he continued to drive himself to develop the Spitfire prototype.

Mitchell was motivated by a visit to Germany in 1934, where he observed the production of military hardware by the Nazis. He was familiar with the Dornier, Heinkel, and Junkers airplanes, and he knew about the Bayerische Flugzeugwerke BF 109 fighter (the ME 109), which was designed by Willy Messerschmitt. Mitchell strongly believed that Britain must respond to the German threat and that Britain needed reliable, high-performance fighters that could be produced in quantity. He drove himself to ensure that his greatest design effort, the Spitfire, would be ready in time to defend England against a German attack.

On March 5, 1936, Spitfire prototype K5054 flew for the first time, piloted by chief test pilot J. "Mutt" Summers from the Eastleigh Airport in Hampshire. Mitchell watched his airplane perform. He knew his perseverance had been rewarded, and that he had accomplished what he had set out to do—to develop a revolutionary, high-performance fighter for which a critical need existed.

Having a high-performance aircraft was crucial for England in the late 1930s, when conflict was increasingly seen as unavoidable. The two principal British fighter aircraft in World War II were the Spitfire and the Hawker Hurricane, which was designed by Sidney Camm. The Hurricane was actually a monoplane version of the Hawker Fury biplane that Camm had designed earlier. The Hurricane was more of a traditional aircraft in that it was built of wood and fabric and stiffened by tubular metal framework. Surprisingly, the fabric-covered fuselage survived cannon shells better than the metal-skinned Spitfire.

The Hurricane was a design halfway between the biplanes of the 1930s and the aircraft design of the 1940s, such as the Spitfire. In the Battle of Britain, the Hurricanes actually downed more German aircraft than the Spitfires, because of the way they were deployed. The faster Spitfires were assigned to engage the German fighters escorting their bombers. The Hurricanes, although slower than the Spitfires, provided an excellent gun platform for attacking the German bombers.

The ME 109 was the leading German fighter; it had similar flight characteristics to the Spitfire. The ME 109 had a tighter turning radius than the Spitfire, but the pilots rarely used this advantage because the ME 109's wings weren't strong enough to withstand the stress of tight turns. The visibility provided by the Spitfire's bubble canopy was superior to the ME 109, whose view to the rear was blocked by the fuselage. Also, the Spitfire pilot had the advantage of armor plate behind his seat.

Mitchell died in June 1937, at the age of forty-two; he never fully regained his strength after his operation in 1933. His condition worsened in early 1937, and his wife, Florence, accompanied him on a visit to a specialist in Austria; however, his cancer was too advanced to operate again. He returned to Southampton, where he died at his home.

The importance of Mitchell's design efforts should not be underestimated. A high-performance fighter, such as the Spitfire, was critically needed in the Battle of Britain to counter Germany's high-performance ME 109. By winning the Battle of Britain, England prevented Hitler's planned invasion across the English channel, and Hitler turned his attention to Russia.

Mitchell's drive and perseverance in pushing the development of the Spitfire while his health was failing resulted in an important contribution to Britain's war effort. It is virtually certain that Mitchell would have received a knighthood for his design efforts had he lived, as Sir Sidney Camm did for his design of the Hawker Hurricane.

* * *

The difficulty with Mitchell's attempts to produce the Spitfire for the Royal Air Force in the late 1930s can be partially explained by Britain's head in the sand attitude about the coming war with Germany. Who can forget Neville Chamberlain's "Peace in our time." It is amazing that the initial development of the Spitfire as a high-performance interceptor was funded by a wealthy widow. The Spitfire was the only British plane that could challenge the ME 109. The fabric-covered Hurricane wasn't as fast or as maneuverable as the Spitfire. Mitchell should have fought harder for financing for his creation, but his health was failing toward the final days of the development of the Spitfire. His company, Supermarine, could have made more of a fight in Parliament for funding for earlier development of the high-performance aircraft.

CHAPTER 16

Chester Carlson (1906-1968) Inventor of Xerography

"Now, through the use of the copying machine, the twenty-five page document can be reproduced in a manner of minutes, and one can have as many copies as one desires. This is true in every profession, in every business, in government agencies in colleges and hospitals and institutions of all sorts, whenever people communicate with written words or charts or pictures. That is why Chester F. Carlson's invention has so often been called one of the most significant of our age."

John Dessauer, *My Years With Xerox, The Billions Nobody Wanted*

Chester Carlson began experimenting with a dry copy process in 1935, and, on October 22, 1938, he produced the first crude copy using his electrophotography process. Carlson, whose job involved processing patents, filed a comprehensive patent in 1939. He spent five years looking for a sponsor to finance the further development and commercialization of his new technology. Over those years, he was turned down by the National Inventors' Council, the U.S. Army Signal Corps, and thirty-two companies, including A. B. Dick, Eastman Kodak, IBM (twice), General Electric, and Remington-Rand (UNIVAC). Carlson said that they all displayed "an enthusiastic lack of interest."

In 1944, Carlson found a sponsor, the Battelle Memorial Institute of Columbus, Ohio. Battelle was to receive sixty percent of future proceeds in return for helping to develop the technology. They suggested the use of selenium instead of sulphur in the process and the use of a specific black toner powder. They, too, were unsuccessful in promoting the product. An Ohio State University professor renamed the process "xerography," from the Greek words "xeros," meaning dry, and "graphos," meaning writing.

Finally, John Dessauer of the Haloid Corporation of Rochester, New York, saw an article about electrophotography in *Radio News*. Dessauer's boss, Joe Wilson, Jr., wanted to increase the $100,000 yearly earnings of the company and had asked him to read technical journals to look for new products or processes. Haloid Corporation purchased the patent and rights to Carlson's technology from Battelle. They produced a flat plate copier in 1949 that required 3-5 minutes per copy, spent more on research and development than they earned each year, and, by 1956, received forty percent of their sales from xerography. The name of the company was changed to Haloid-Xerox.

In 1959, IBM was asked to manufacture copiers for Haloid-Xerox. IBM commissioned Arthur D. Little, a consultant from Cambridge, Massachusetts, to do a study of the market potential. The study identified a total potential market of 5,000 units of sales for Haloid-Xerox's new 914 copier. IBM declined the offer to participate in Xerography a second time, and Haloid-Xerox began to manufacture the model 914 copier themselves. By 1968, they had produced 200,000 of them. The fallacy in the Arthur D. Little study was in basing their recommendations on the estimate of the number of copies made at the point of origin, using the original. Most copies are made at the point of receipt from copies made elsewhere.

Haloid-Xerox changed its name to the Xerox Corporation in 1961. By 1988, three billion copies were being made each day worldwide, and the business of making copies had become a $22 billion a year business. The technology that nobody wanted made millionaires out of many people and revolutionized the way in which we communicate with one another.

* * *

The failure to recognize the potential of the copier is another amazing example of lost opportunity. One cannot solely fault Carlson for not attempting to promote his product. He approached many large corporations over a period of years and a highly regarded consulting firm was contracted. It may be hindsight, but he could have approached medium-sized companies and even small companies with R & D funds, which was where he finally met with success with the Haloid Corporation.

EPILOGUE

Improving Emotional Intelligence

"The most exciting and promising aspect of Emotional Intelligence is that we are able to change it. In other words, unlike our IQ, we are not stuck with what we are born with. The great news about EQ is that it is not fixed or only developed at a certain stage of life. It has been shown that life experiences can be used to increase our EQ and that we can continue to develop our capacity to learn and adapt as we grow older. The EQ realm is one area that does reward us for successfully having gone through stages of our lives."

Harvey Deutschendorf, *The Other Kind of Smart*

The place to begin in increasing one's Emotional Intelligence is self-awareness, knowing oneself, particularly strengths and weaknesses. A positive self-regard is important. We should stay positive, even when discussing our weaknesses. For example, if someone asks about our impatience, we can admit to being impatient but that we are working on it, and it is getting better.

In choosing the area to begin with in increasing your Emotional Intelligence, pick the area in which you have the most to gain. Improvement cannot be expected to occur overnight. For many people, working on controlling their impulses, not saying the first thing that comes to their minds, will come first.

In *People Smart,* Mel Silberman has listed skills that can be worked on and improved, including:

- Expressing Yourself Clearly—get the message across
- Asserting Your Needs—be straightforward but establish limits
- Exchanging Feedback—be descriptive without giving offense
- Influencing Others—be able to motivate others
- Resolving Conflict—define problems and suggest solutions
- Being a Team Player—build consensus
- Shifting Gears—be flexible and resilient

In *Emotional Intelligence Works,* S. Michael Kravitz and Susan D. Schubert list skills that can be more fully developed, including:

- Improve Your Listening Skills
- Adapt to the Communication Needs of Others
- [Learn How to] Confront Negative People
- Develop Social Skills
- Foster Optimism
- Encourage Flexibility and Problem Solving
- Model and Encourage Emotional Control
- Support Teamwork

Extroverts tend to have more people smarts than introverts. Nevertheless, we can all improve our people skills. Self-assessment surveys can be helpful in establishing the starting point of our efforts to improve our Emotional Intelligence.

In 1980, Reuven Bar-On developed a test to measure Emotional Intelligence. The BarOnEQ-i, or Emotional Quotient Inventory, has been approved by the American Psychological Association.

In 1990, John Mayer, Peter Salovey, and David Caruso developed the Mayer-Salovey-Caruso Emotional Intelligence Test (MSCEIT). It is an ability-based test of Emotional Intelligence.

These tests may be helpful in a program to increase Emotional Intelligence. Anyone desiring to improve his or her chances of achieving success will be motivated to spend the time and the effort.

As stated earlier, a purpose of this book is to provide role models of Emotional Intelligence from history from whom we can learn skills to aid in increasing our EQ. For a more comprehensive discussion of Emotional Intelligence and how to increase EQ, works by authors quoted in this book are highly recommended.

What Constitutes Success

"He has achieved success who has lived well, laughed often, and loved much; who has gained the respect of intelligent men and the love of little children; who has filled his niche and accomplished his task; who has left the world better than he found it, whether by an improved poppy, a perfect poem, or a rescued soul; who has never lacked appreciation of earth's beauty or failed to express it; who has looked for the best in others and given the best he had; whose life was an inspiration; whose memory is a benediction."

Mrs. A. J. "Bessie" Stanley

BIBLIOGRAPHY

Ackerman, Carl W. *George Eastman.*
Clifton, NJ: Augustus M. Kelly, 1973.

Andrews, Linda Wasner. *Emotional Intelligence.* New York:
Franklin Watts, 2004.

Arrington, Leonard J. *Brigham Young: American Moses.*
New York: Alfred A. Knopf, 1985.

Baker, George, ed. *The Life of William H. Seward
with Selections from His Works.* New York: Redfield, 1855.

Baker, Nina Brown. *Robert Bruce, King of Scots.*
New York: Vanguard, 1948.

Bar-On, Reuven, J.G. Maree, and Maurice Jesse Elias, eds.
Educating People to Be Emotionally Intelligent. Westport, CT:
Praeger, 2007.

Barchilon, John. *The Crown Prince.* New York: Norton, 1984.

Barker, Dudley. "Mrs. Emmeline Pankhurst,"
Prominent Edwardians. New York: Athenaeum, 1969.

Bebre, Patrice. *Louis Pasteur.* Baltimore:
Johns Hopkins University Press, 1998.

Bennett, Geoffrey Martin. *Nelson the Commander.*
New York: Scribner's, 1972.

Bobbé, Dorothie. *DeWitt Clinton.* New York: Putnam, 1968.

Boslough, John. *Stephen Hawking's Universe.* New York: Avon,
1985.

Brabazon, James. *Albert Schweitzer: A Biography.*
London: Victor Gollancz, 1976.

Branden, Nathaniel. *Six Pillars of Self-Esteem.* New York:
Bantam, 1994.

Brayer, Elizabeth. *George Eastman: A Biography.*
Baltimore: Johns Hopkins University Press, 1996.

Brickhill, Paul. *Reach for the Sky: The Story of Douglas Bader,
Legless Ace of the Battle of Britain.* New York: Norton, 1954.

Bringhurst, Newell G. *Brigham Young and the Expanding
American Frontier.* Boston: Little, Brown, 1986.

Brown, Jared. *The Fabulous Lunts: A Biography of Alfred Lunt and
Lynn Fontanne.* New York: Athenaeum, 1986.

Bryant, Arthur. *The Great Duke.* New York: Morrow, 1972.

Burks, Alice R., and Arthur W. Burks. *The First Electronic
Computer: The Atanasoff Story.* Ann Arbor:
University of Michigan Press, 1989.

Casper, Christine Mockler. *From Now On with Passion: A Guide to Emotional Intelligence.* New York: Cypress House, 2001.

Castle, Barbara. *Sylvia and Christabel Pankhurst.* New York: Penguin, 1987.

Collier, Richard. *Eagle Day: The Battle of Britain, August 6—September 15, 1940.* New York: Dutton, 1966.

Cooper, Robert K., and Ayman Sawaf. *Executive EQ: Emotional Intelligence in Leadership and Organizations.* New York: Grosset / Putnam, 1997.

Cousins, Norman. *Dr. Schweitzer of Lambarene.* New York: Harper & Brothers, 1960.

Cushnir, Raphael. *The One Thing Holding You Back: Unleashing the Power of Emotional Connection.* New York: Harper, 2008.

Dessauer, John H. *My Years With Xerox: The Billions Nobody Wanted.* Garden City, NY: Doubleday. 1971.

Deutschendorf, Harvey. *The Other Kind of Smart.* New York: Amacom, 2009.

Dorf, Philip. *The Builder: A Biography of Ezra Cornell.* New York: Macmillan, 1952.

Dubos. Rene. *Pasteur and Modern Science.* Madison, WI: Science Tech, 1960.

Ferguson, Kitty. *Stephen Hawking: Quest for a Theory of the Universe.* New York: Franklin Watts, 1991.

Flindell, E. Fred. "Paul Wittgenstein (1887-1961): Patron and Pianist." *The Music Review,* xxxi, 1971.

Forster, Margaret. *Elizabeth Barrett Browning: A Biography.* New York: Doubleday, 1988.

Gardner, Howard. *Multiple Intelligences: The Theory in Practice.* New York: Basic Books, 1993.

Geddes, George. *Origin and History of the Measures that Led to the Construction of the Erie Canal.* Syracuse: Sommers, 1866.

Geisen, Gerald L. *The Private Science of Louis Pasteur.* Princeton: Princeton University Press, 1995.

Goleman, Daniel. *Emotional Intelligence: Why It Can Matter More Than IQ.* New York: Bantam Books, 1995.

—.*Working with Emotional Intelligence.* New York: Bantam Books, 1998.

Hawking, Stephen W. *A Brief History of Time: From the Big Bang to Black Holes.* New York: Bantam, 1988.

Hendrickson, Robert. *The Grand Emporiums.*
New York: Stein & Day, 1979.

Hoobler, Dorothy and Thomas. *Nelson and Winnie Mandela.*
New York: Franklin Watts, 1987.

Hough, Richard. *The Battle of Britain: The Triumph of R.A.F.*
Fighter Pilots. New York: Macmillan, 1971.

Hungerford, Edward. *The Romance of a Great Store.*
New York: McBride, 1922.

Hylander, C. J. *American Inventors.* New York: Macmillan, 1958.

Jahoda, Gloria. *The Road To Samarkand: Frederick Delius*
and His Music. New York: Charles Scribner's Sons, 1969.

Karlin, Daniel. *The Courtship of Robert Browning and*
Elizabeth Barrett. Oxford: Clarenden, 1985.

Klees, Emerson. *The Drive to Succeed: Role Models of Motivation.*
Rochester, NY: Cameo Press, 2002.

—. *Entrepreneurs in History—Success vs. Failure:*
Entrepreneurial Role Models. Rochester, NY: Cameo Press,
1995.

—. *One Plus One Equals Three—Pairing Man / Woman Strengths.*
Rochester, NY: Friends of the Finger Lakes Publishing, 1998.

—. *Staying With It: Role Models of Perseverance.* Rochester, NY:
Cameo Press, 1999.

—. *The Will To Stay With It: Role Models of Determination.*
Rochester, NY: Cameo Press, 2002.

Kravitz, S. Michael, and Susan D. Schubert. *Emotional Intelligence*
Works: Developing People Smart Strategies. Menlo Park, CA:
Crisp Learning, 2000.

Lader, Lawrence. *The Margaret Sanger Story and the Fight*
for Birth Control. Garden City: Doubleday, 1955.

Lader Lawrence, and Milton Meltzer. *Margaret Sanger:*
Pioneer of Birth Control. New York: Crowell, 1968.

Longford, Elizabeth. *Wellington: The Years of the Sword.*
New York: Harper & Row, 1969.

Mandela, Nelson. *Long Walk To Freedom.* Boston: Little, Brown,
1994.

Markus, Julia. *Dared and Done: The Marriage of Elizabeth Barrett*
Browning and Robert Browning. NY: Alfred A. Knopf, 1965.

Maslow, Abraham H. *Motivation and Personality.* New York:
Harper & Row, 1970.

Matthews, Gerald, Moshe Zeidner, and Robert D. Roberts.
Emotional Intelligence: Science and Myth. Cambridge, MA:
MIT Press, 2002.

Mitchell, David. *The Fighting Pankhursts: A Study in Tenacity.*
New York: Macmillan, 1967.

Mollenkoff, Clark R. *Atanasoff: Forgotten Father of the Computer.*
Ames, Iowa: Iowa State University Press, 1988.

Oman, Carola. *Nelson.* Garden City, NY: Doubleday, 1946.

Pankhurst, E. Sylvia. *The Life of Emmeline Pankhurst:
The Suffragette Struggle for Women's Citizenship.*
Boston: Houghton Mifflin, 1936.

Reynolds, Moira Davison. *How Pasteur Changed History.*
Bradenton, FL: McGuinn & McGuire, 1974.

Robbins, David. *Men of Honor.* New York: Onyx, 2000.

Sanger, Margaret. *An Autobiography.* New York: Norton, 1938.

Schweitzer, Albert. *Out of My Life and Thought:
An Autobiography.* New York: Henry Holt, 1933.

Scott, Sir Walter. "History of Scotland," *Tales of a Grandfather.*
Boston: Tichnor and Fields, 1861.

Segal, Jeanne. *Raising Your Emotional Intelligence:
A Practical Guide.* New York: Henry Holt, 1997.

Seligman, Martin E. P. *Learned Optimism.* New York:
Alfred A. Knopf, 1991.

Silberman, Mel. *People Smart.* San Francisco: Berrett-Koehler,
2000.

Smiley, Jane. *The Man Who Invented the Computer.*
New York: Doubleday, 2010.

Smith, Douglas K. and Robert C. Alexander. *Fumbling the Future.*
New York: William Morrrow, 1988.

Southey, Robert. *Life of Nelson.* New York: Dutton, 1813.

Stack, V. E., ed. *How Do I Love Thee? The Love-Letters of
Robert Browning and Elizabeth Barrett.* New York:
G. Putnam's Sons, 1969.

Stein, Steven J., and Howard E. Book. *The EQ Edge:
Emotional Intelligence and Your Success.* Toronto, Canada:
John Wiley & Sons, 1996.

Stillwell, Paul. *The Reminiscences of Master Chief Carl M.
Brashear, U.S. Navy.* Annapolis: U.S. Naval Institute, 1998.

Taves, Ernest H. *This Is the Place: Brigham and the New Zion.*
Buffalo: Prometheus Books, 1991.

Thomas, Donald. *Robert Browning: A Life Within Life.*
London: Weidenfeld and Nicolson, 1982.

Topalian, Elysse. *Margaret Sanger.* New York: Franklin Watts,
1984.

Townsend, Peter. *Duel of Eagles.* New York: Simon & Schuster,
1970.

Torvill, Jayne, and Christopher Dean with John Man. *Torvill &
Dean: The Autobiography of Ice Dancing's Greatest Stars.*
Secaucus, NJ: Carol Publishing, 1996.

Tranter, Nigel. *Robert the Bruce: The Path of the Hero King.*
New York: St. Martin's, 1970.

Untermeyer, Louis. *Makers of the Modern World.*
New York: Simon & Schuster, 1955.

Valerie-Radot, Rene. *The Life of Louis Pasteur.*
Garden City, NY: Sun Dial Press, 1937.

Vail, John. *Nelson and Winnie Mandela.* New York:
Chelsea House, 1989.

Van Deusen, Glyndon G. *William Henry Seward.*
New York: Oxford University Press, 1967.

Ward, Stephen George. *Wellington.* New York: Arco, 1963.

Warlock, Peter (Philip Heseltine). *Frederick Delius.*
New York: Oxford University Press, 1952.

Warner, Oliver. *Victory, The Life of Lord Nelson.*
Boston: Little, Brown, 1958.

Weisinger, Hendrie. *Emotional Intelligence at Work: The Untapped
Edge for Success.* San Francisco: Jossey-Bass, 1998.

White, Michael and John Gribben. *Stephen Hawking:
A Life in Science,* Minneapolis: Dutton, 1992.

Wilkinson, Clennell. *Nelson.* London: Harrop, 1931.

Winwar, Frances. *The Immortal Lovers: Elizabeth and
Robert Browning.* New York: Harper & Brothers, 1950.

Zeidner, Moshe, Gerald Matthews, and Richard D. Booth.
What We Know about Emotional Intelligence. Cambridge, MA:
MIT Press, 2009.

Zolotow, Maurice. *Stagestruck: The Romance of Alfred Lunt and
Lynn Fontanne.* New York: Harcourt, Brace & World, 1965.